modern BABY crochet

18 crocheted baby garments, blankets, accessories, and more!

SHARON ZIENTARA

 INTERWEAVE.
interweave.com

Contents

4 INTRODUCTION

6 THE PROJECTS

6 Octavia the Octopus Rattle
Brenda K. B. Anderson

12 Dylan Hoodie
Anastasia Popova

18 Lily Leg Warmers
Janet Brani

22 Oliver Cabled Earflap Hat
A la Sascha

26 Claire Dress
Kathy Merrick

34 Parker Pants
Sharon Zientara

40 Cameron Blanket
Cristina Mershon

44 Zoe the Cat Slippers
Brenda K. B. Anderson

50 Liam Zippered Pullover
Robyn Chachula

64 Oskar Car Seat Swaddle
Terri L. Keller

72 Ladybug the Dachshund Sweater
Brenda K. B. Anderson

80 Finley the Fox Bib
Lisa van Klaveren

84 Eddy Burp Cloths
Brenda K. B. Anderson

90 Spike the Hedgehog Hat
Brenda K. B. Anderson

98 Sophie Raglan Pullover
Katya Novikova

104 Landon Faux Cabled Pullover
Robyn Chachula

112 Ava Cloth Diaper Wrap
Anastasia Popova

116 Charlie Booties
Sharon Zientara

120 ABBREVIATIONS

120 GLOSSARY

124 SOURCES FOR YARNS

124 ACKNOWLEDGMENTS

125 ABOUT THE DESIGNERS

126 INDEX

Introduction

In this, the latest addition of the 3 Skeins or Less series, we thought it only fitting that we focus on some of the cutest, most crochet-worthy people in our lives—babies! The three skeins or less concept is perfectly suited to baby projects because little ones grow so quickly. The faster a baby item is to make, the longer he or she can wear it! Each one of the patterns you'll find here is handpicked for maximum cuteness, as well as how fun it is to make.

Baby projects are great opportunities to hone your crochet skills. If you are a new or intermediate crocheter, there are plenty of interesting techniques in each pattern, but in a tiny, less intimidating project. We also included a few fantastic little sweaters, and if you're thinking about dipping your toe into garment making, these are great patterns to help ease you into it and teach you some valuable lessons. Of course, if all you're looking for is an adorable group of patterns to crochet for the wee ones in your life, we have plenty of those. Whatever the reason you pick up this book, enjoy making something special for some very sweet recipients.

Octavia the Octopus
RATTLE

DESIGNED BY BRENDA K. B. ANDERSON

Most babies have lots of stuffed animals but few as special and unique as this darling little handmade octopus. This sweet friend takes just one skein of yarn and has the versatility to be a cuddly toy and a stimulating rattle. Either way, Octavia is a toy that baby is sure to love.

FINISHED SIZE
Model shown measures about 5½" (14 cm) tall and head measures about 10¾" (27.5 cm) in circumference after stuffing with polyester stuffing.

YARN
DK weight (#3 Light).

Shown here: Berroco Weekend DK (75% acrylic, 25% Peruvian cotton; 268 yd [247 m]/3½ oz [100 g]): #2983 Cottage, 1 skein.

HOOKS
Size E/4 (3.5 mm) and steel hook size 6 (1.6 mm). Adjust hook size if necessary to obtain correct gauge.

NOTIONS
Stitch markers (m); yarn needle; polyester stuffing; small amounts of black and white felt (for eyes); black and white sewing thread and needle; sewing pins; black embroidery floss; embroidery needle; 2 squares of fabric or 1 square of felt that measures about 9" × 9" (23 × 23 cm) (optional; for bottom appliqué); matching thread (for appliqué); 1 small plastic container with lid that holds about 1.18 oz (35 ml); ½ oz (14 g) bag of poly pellets (or something that makes noise—see Notes); superglue (optional, for plastic container lid).

GAUGE
20 sts and 16 rnds = 4" (10 cm) in esc worked in the rnd. To make a gauge swatch, work through Rnd 6 of head instructions. Circle should measure 3" (7.5 cm) in diameter.

NOTES
Octavia is crocheted in two pieces and then slip-stitched together after stuffing.

Mouth and outline around eyes (including eyelashes) are crocheted bits of embroidery floss that are sewn onto Octavia's face.

Hidden inside Octavia's head is a tiny plastic container filled with poly pellet beads (plastic pellets) to make a little noise when she dances. This container must be small enough so that it can fit inside Octavia's head with space around it to stuff with polyester stuffing. A Sistema brand 1.18 oz (35 ml) dressing container is used here with 1 Tbsp (½ oz) of poly pellets. Make sure lid is fastened well. Use dab of superglue to make sure it won't come off.

Octavia has an optional contrasting appliqué stitched to her underside, but if you prefer, you can omit appliqué and make her crocheted underside out of a contrasting-color yarn instead.

Underside

Rnd 1: Using larger hook, make an adjustable ring (see Glossary), 8 esc (see Stitch Guide) in ring, pull on beg tail to close ring—8 sts. Do not join, but work in a spiral.

Rnd 2: 2 esc in each st—16 sts. Place marker (pm) to keep track of beg of rnds.

Rnd 3: [2 esc in next st, esc in next st] 8 times—24 sts.

Rnd 4: [Esc in next st, 2 esc in next st, esc in next st] 8 times—32 sts.

Rnd 5: [Esc in next 2 sts, ch 13, beg with 2nd ch from hook (first ch from hook does not count as st) and working in bottom of ch, esc in next 12 ch, continuing to work in sts from Rnd 5, esc in next 2 sts] 8 times—224 sts around including bottom side of foundation ch, 8 spokes sticking out from center circle.

Rnd 6: [Esc in next 13 sts, 3 esc in next st, sk turning ch, working into opposite side of spoke, 3 esc in next st, esc in next 13 sts] 8 times—256 sts.

Note: There are sc as well as esc used in the next 2 rnds.

Rnd 7: [Esc in next 2 sts, 2 esc in next 2 sts, esc in next 4 sts, [esc2tog] twice (see Stitch Guide), esc in next st, sc in next 2 sts, 3 sc in next 2 sts, sc in next 2 sts, esc in next st, [esc2tog] twice, esc in next 4 sts, 2 esc in next 2 sts, esc in next 2 sts] 8 times—288 sts.

Rnd 8: [Esc in next 10 sts, sc in next 2 sts, sc2tog (see Glossary), sc in next 8 sts, sc2tog, sc in next 2 sts, esc in next 10 sts] 8 times—272 sts. Sl st in first st of rnd. Fasten off. Pm in first st of rnd. Set aside.

Head/Top Surface of Legs

Rnd 1: Using larger hook, make an adjustable ring, 8 esc in ring, pull on beg tail to close ring—8 sts. Do not join, but work in a spiral.

Rnd 2: 2 esc in each st—16 sts. Pm to keep track of beg of rnds.

Rnd 3: [2 esc in next st, esc in next st] 8 times—24 sts.

Rnd 4: [Esc in next st, 2 esc in next st, esc in next st] 8 times—32 sts.

Rnd 5: [Esc in next 3 sts, 2 esc in next st] 8 times—40 sts.

Rnd 6: [Esc in next 4 sts, 2 esc in next st, esc in next 5 sts] 4 times—44 sts. Diameter should measure 3" (7.5 cm).

Rnd 7: [2 esc in next st, esc in next 10 sts] 4 times—48 sts.

Rnd 8: [Esc in next 5 sts, 2 esc in next st, esc in next 6 sts] 4 times—52 sts.

Rnds 9-12: Esc in each st around.

Rnds 13-16: Work in esc decreasing 2 sts each rnd. Place decreases in different location each rnd; avoid making an esc2tog stitch into another esc2tog st from previous round—44 sts after working Rnd 16.

Rnds 17-20: Work in esc working 4 evenly spaced esc2tog stitches around, making sure to stagger decreases in subsequent rnds so they are not directly on top of one another—28 sts after Rnd 20.

Place some stuffing into Octavia's head, insert plastic container, and stuff around sides of container.

Rnd 21: Esc in each st around.

Rnd 22: [Esc in next 6 sts, 2 esc in next st] 4 times—32 sts.

Rnd 23: [Esc in next 2 sts, ch 15, beg with 2nd ch from hook (first ch from hook does not count as st) and working in bottom of ch, esc in next 14 ch sts, continuing to work in sts from Rnd 22, esc in next 2 sts] 8 times—256 sts around including bottom side of foundation ch, 8 spokes sticking out from center.

Rnd 24: [Esc2tog, esc in next 8 sts, sc in next 5 sts, 3 sc in next st, sk turning ch, working into opposite side of spoke, 3 sc in next st, sc in next 5 sts, esc in next 8 sts, esc2tog] 8 times—272 sts. Do not fasten off.

Place underside behind rnd just worked with WS tog. Beg with next st of Rnd 24 and marked st of underside, sl st layers tog by working sl sts through both layers at same time. Stuff Octavia with polyester stuffing as you work your way around each leg. Fasten off.

Eye Outline/Eyelashes (make 2)

Using steel hook and embroidery floss, ch 13, beg with 2nd ch from hook and working in bottom of ch, sl st in next 3 ch, ch 5, beg with 2nd ch from hook and working in bottom ch, sl st in next 3 ch, ch 9. Check to make sure that this is long enough to go around edge of eye white. If not, make more ch until it is long enough. Fasten off, leaving long tail for sewing.

Mouth

Using steel hook and embroidery floss, ch 7, beg with 2nd ch from hook and working in bottom of ch, sl st in next 2 ch, sc in next 2 sc, sl st in next 2 ch—6 sts. Fasten off, leaving long tail for sewing.

Finishing

Cut 2 each of eye whites and black pupils out of felt using template. Pin eye whites to face using photos as a guide. Using sewing needle and white thread, whipstitch (see Glossary)

around edge of each eye white. Pin pupils to eye whites using photos as a guide. Take time when placing pupils onto eye whites; the slightest change in position will change her expression significantly. Using sewing needle and black thread, whipstitch each pupil to eye white. Pin eye outlines/eyelashes in place around eye whites. Sew in place using tails of embroidery floss and embroidery needle. Pin mouth in place and stitch to face using tails and embroidery floss. Weave in ends.

Note: If Octavia's neck is thicker than you would like after stuffing, or if you can see stuffing between stitches and would like to close gaps between them, just thread a yarn needle with a long piece of yarn and weave through three rnds of Octavia's neck to pull it a bit tighter. Be sure to hide strand of yarn within sts; yarn needle should be mostly on inside of neck as you work, just catching backs of sts as you slide needle from one st to next.

APPLIQUÉ (OPTIONAL)

The sample shown here has a fabric appliqué bottom. You can also make a bottom out of felt.

Fabric Bottom

Using template, trace out appliqué on WS of one of the squares of fabric. This will be the stitching line. Cut a hole in center of traced appliqué that is about the size of a nickel. Place other square of fabric behind, with RS facing, and pin in place. Using sewing thread and needle, stitch around edges of appliqué along traced stitching line. Trim around appliqué leaving a 3/8" (1 cm) seam allowance. Clip through seam allowance in each "valley" between legs. Be careful not to clip through sts, but the closer you can get to the stitching line, the easier it will be to turn each leg RS out. Make little V-shaped cutouts in seam allowance along curves at tip of each leg. Again, be very careful not to cut through thread. In order to help turn appliqué RS out, using scissors, make a long slice from center hole toward tip of each leg. Stop short of tip by about 3/4" (2 cm). Turn RS out and press

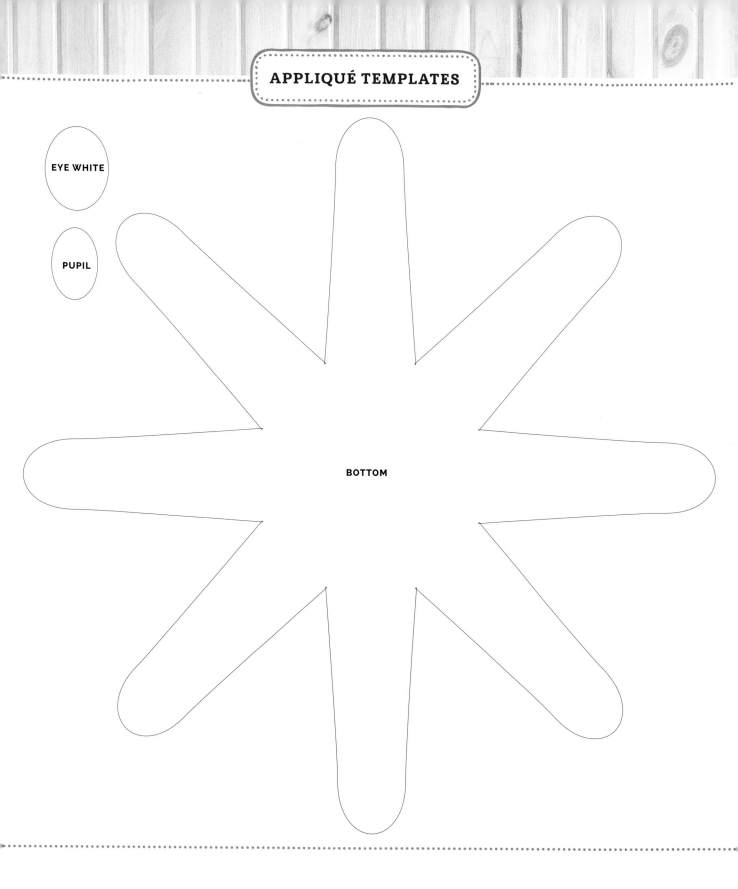

EYE WHITE

PUPIL

BOTTOM

with iron. Pin to underside of Octavia and using sewing needle and thread, whipstitch all the way around edges to secure in place.

Felt Bottom
Using template, trace out appliqué on felt square and cut along this line. Pin to underside of Octavia and using sewing needle and thread, whipstitch all the way around edges to secure in place.

Dylan
HOODIE

DESIGNED BY ANASTASIA POPOVA

This comfy cardigan makes a great layering piece for any baby boy or girl. The construction is kept simple, so you can enjoy the twisting of the cables and special design touches like the sporty hood and sewn-in zipper.

FINISHED SIZE

Instructions are written for size 3–6 months. Changes for 6–12 months, 12–18 months, and 18–24 months are in parentheses.

Chest circumference: 23½ (25½, 27¼, 29)" (59.5 [65, 69, 73.5] cm).

Shown in size 3–6 months.

YARN

DK weight (#3 Light).

Shown here: Hazel Knits Artisan Lively DK (90% superwash merino, 10% nylon; 275 yd [251 m]/4½ oz [130 g]): fresh cut, 3 skeins.

HOOK

Size G/6 (4 mm). Adjust hook size if necessary to obtain correct gauge.

NOTIONS

Stitch markers (m); yarn needle; 8 (10, 10, 12)" (20.5 [25.5, 25.5, 30.5] cm) separating zipper; sewing thread in color to match zipper; sewing needle; sewing pins.

GAUGE

13 sts and 7 rows = 3" (7.5 cm) in linked double crochet (see Stitch Guide).

NOTES

The hood is made first, then raglan increases are made. Sleeves are separated, and body is worked from underarms down. Then the sleeves are crocheted flat and seamed.

Beg linked double crochet (beg-ldc): Insert hook in 2nd ch from hook, yo and pull up lp, insert hook in next st, yo and pull up lp (3 lps on hook), [yo and draw through 2 lps] 2 times.

Linked double crochet (ldc): Insert hook in horizontal bar of last st made, yo and pull up lp, insert hook into next st, yo and pull up lp (3 lps on hook), [yo and draw through 2 lps] 2 times.

Front post treble crochet (FPtr): Yo 2 times, insert hook from front to back to front around the post of specified st, yo and pull up lp, [yo and draw through 2 lps on hook] 3 times.

Back post treble crochet (BPtr): Yo 2 times, insert hook from back to front to back around the post of specified st, yo and pull up lp, [yo and draw through 2 lps on hook] 3 times.

Front post double treble crochet (FPdtr): Yo 3 times, insert hook from front to back to front around the post of specified st, yo and pull up lp, [yo and draw through 2 lps on hook] 4 times.

Cluster (CL): [Yo twice, insert hook in next st, yo and pull up lp, (yo and draw through 2 lps on hook) twice] 4 times, yo, draw through all 5 lps on hook.

CABLE PATTERN (WORKED OVER 9 STS)
Row 1: (RS) Ldc in next 2 sts, sk next 3 sts, FPdtr in next 2 sts, dc in last st of 3 skipped sts, working in front of sts just made, FPdtr in skipped 2 sts, dc in next st, ldc in next st.

Row 2: Ldc in next st, skip next st, BPtr in next post st, BPtr/dc in next post st, dc in next st, dc/BPtr in next post st, BPtr in next post st, sk next st, dc in next st.

Row 3: Sk next st, FPtr in next post st, FPtr/dc in next post st, dc in next st, CL in next st, dc in next st, dc/FPtr in next post st, FPtr in next post st, sk next st.

Row 4: Dc/BPtr in next post st, BPtr in next post st, sk next st, dc in next 3 sts, sk next st, BPtr in next post st, BPtr/dc in next post st.

Row 5: Ldc in next 2 sts, sk next 4 sts, FPdtr in next 2 sts, dc in 3rd st of 4 skipped sts, working in front of sts just made, FPdtr in 2 skipped post sts, dc in last post st, ldc in next st.

Row 6: Ldc in next 2 sts, BPtr in next 2 post sts, dc in next dc, BPtr in next 2 post sts, dc in next st, ldc in next st.

Hood
Ch 21 (23, 26, 28).

Row 1: (WS) Beg-ldc in 3rd ch from hook, ldc in next 2 sts, dc in next 6 sts, ldc in each ch to last ch, 6 ldc in last ch. Working on opposite side of foundation ch, ldc in each ch to last 9 ch, dc in next 6 ch, ldc in each ch across, turn—42 (46, 52, 56) sts.

Row 2: Ch 2 (counts as ldc), ldc in next st, work Row 1 of cable pattern over next 9 sts, pm in last st, ldc in next 7 (9, 12, 14) sts, 2 ldc in next st, ldc in next st, 2 ldc in each of next 2 sts, ldc in next st, 2 ldc in next st, ldc in next 7 (9, 12, 14) sts, work Row 1 of cable pattern over next 9 sts, ldc in next 2 sts, turn—46 (50, 56, 60) sts. Move marker up as work progresses.

Row 3: Ch 2, ldc in next st, work next row of cable pattern, pm in last st, ldc in next 7 (9, 12, 14) sts, 2 ldc in next st, [ldc in next 2 sts, 2 ldc in next st] 3 times, ldc in each st to next m, work next row of cable pattern, ldc in next 2 sts, turn—50 (54, 60, 64) sts.

Move marker up as work progresses.

Row 4: Ch 2, ldc in next st, work next row of cable pattern, dc in next st, ldc in each st to next m, work next row of cable pattern, dc in next st, ldc in next st, turn.

Row 5: Ch 2, ldc in next st, work next row of cable pattern, ldc in each st to next m, work next row of cable pattern, ldc in next 2 sts, turn.

Cont in cable patt as est, rep Row 5 four times, then Row 4 once, then Row 5 one (four, five, five) times, then Row 4 zero (zero, one, one) time(s), then Row 5 one (one, two, five) time(s).

Next row: Ch 2, ldc in next st, work next row of cable pattern, ldc in next 7 (9, 12, 14) sts, [sk next st, ldc in next 5 sts] twice, sk next st, ldc in each st to next m, work next row of cable pattern, ldc in next 2 sts, turn—47 (51, 57, 61) sts.

Size 3–6 Months only
Next row: Ch 2, ldc in next st, work next row of cable pattern, ldc in next 12 sts, sk next st, ldc in each st to next m, work next row of cable pattern, ldc in next 2 sts—46 sts, do not fasten off, turn.

Next row: Ch 2, ldc in next st, work next row of cable pattern, ldc in next 9 (12, 14) sts, [sk next st, ldc in next 4 sts] twice, sk next st, ldc in each st to next m, work next row of cable pattern, ldc in next 2 sts—48 (54, 58) sts, do not fasten off, turn.

Yoke

Row 1: Ch 2, ldc in next st, work first 7 sts of next row of cable pattern, 5 ldc in next st, ldc in next 3 (4, 7, 9) sts, 5 ldc in next st, ldc in next 18 sts, 5 ldc in next st, ldc in next 3 (4, 7, 9) sts, 5 ldc in next st, work last 7 sts of next row of cable pattern, ldc in next 2 sts, turn—62 (64, 70, 74) sts.

Row 2: Ch 2, ldc in next st, work next row of cable pattern, [ldc in each st to next 3rd st of 5 ldc, 5 ldc in next st] 4 times, ldc in each st to next m, work next row of cable pattern, ldc in next 2 sts, turn—78 (80, 86, 90) sts.

Rep Row 2 five (six, seven, eight) more times—158 (176, 198, 218) sts.

Body

Row 1: Ch 2, ldc in next st, work next row of cable pattern, ldc in next 13 (15, 17, 19) sts, ch 3, sk next 31 (36, 43, 49) sts for sleeve, ldc in next 48 (52, 56, 60) sts, ch 3, sk next 31 (36, 43, 49) sts for sleeve, ldc in each st to next m, work next row of cable pattern, ldc in next 2 sts, turn—102 (110, 118, 126) sts.

Row 2: Ch 2, ldc in next st, work next row of cable pattern, ldc in each st to next m, work next row of cable pattern, ldc in next 2 sts, turn.

Rep Row 2 thirteen (fifteen, seventeen, twenty) more times. Do not fasten off, continue with edging.

Edging (Body and Hood)

Note: While crocheting edging, it's important to make sure that front edge does not become overstretched.

Row 1: Ch 1, sc evenly across row-ends of body and hood (about 5 sc per 3 row-ends).

Row 2: With RS facing (turn if necessary), work 1 row of reverse sc around body, hood, and bottom edges. Fasten off.

Sleeve (make 2)

With RS facing, join yarn in the center of ch-3 at underarm.

Row 1: Ch 2, ldc in next ch, 2 ldc in next row-end, ldc in next 31 (36, 43, 49) sts, 2 ldc in next row-end, ldc in next ch, turn—38 (43, 50, 56) sts.

Row 2: Ch 2, ldc in next st, sk next st, ldc in each st to last 4 sts, sk next st, ldc in next 2 sts, sk turning ch, turn—35 (40, 47, 53) sts.

Row 3: Ch 2, ldc in each st to last st, sk turning ch, turn—34 (39, 46, 52) sts.

Rep Row 3 seven (nine, twelve, fifteen) more times—27 (30, 34, 37) sts. Sl st into turning chain. Do not fasten off.

Next row: With RS facing (turn if necessary), ch 1, rev sc in each st across.

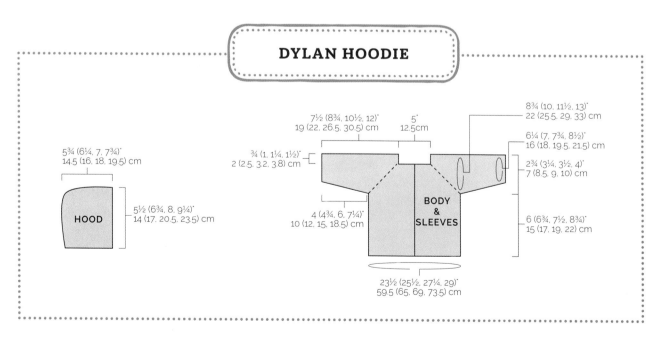

DYLAN HOODIE

5¾ (6¼, 7, 7¾)"
14.5 (16, 18, 19.5) cm

5½ (6¾, 8, 9¼)"
14 (17, 20.5, 23.5) cm

HOOD

7½ (8¾, 10½, 12)"
19 (22, 26.5, 30.5) cm

5"
12.5cm

¾ (1, 1¼, 1½)"
2 (2.5, 3.2, 3.8) cm

4 (4¾, 6, 7¼)"
10 (12, 15, 18.5) cm

BODY & SLEEVES

8¾ (10, 11½, 13)"
22 (25.5, 29, 33) cm

6¼ (7, 7¾, 8½)"
16 (18, 19.5, 21.5) cm

2¾ (3¼, 3½, 4)"
7 (8.5, 9, 10) cm

6 (6¾, 7½, 8¾)"
15 (17, 19, 22) cm

23½ (25½, 27¼, 29)"
59.5 (65, 69, 73.5) cm

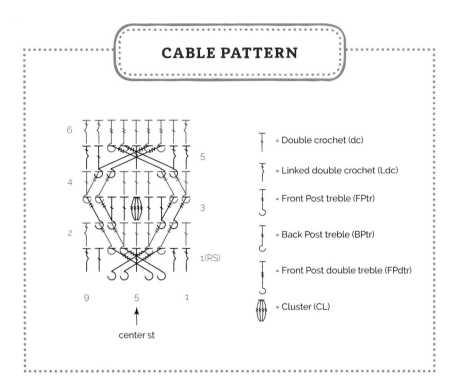

CABLE PATTERN

= Double crochet (dc)

= Linked double crochet (Ldc)

= Front Post treble (FPtr)

= Back Post treble (BPtr)

= Front Post double treble (FPdtr)

= Cluster (CL)

center st

Fasten off, leaving 10" (25.5 cm) tail for sewing.

Finishing

Using yarn needle, seam up sleeve edges. Weave in ends and block hoodie to measurements.

ATTACH ZIPPER

With the RS facing, line up right and left fronts. Place closed zipper under garment allowing teeth and part of zipper to show. Align bottom of zipper with bottom edge of sweater and pin in place; top of zipper should be below Row 2 of yoke. Pin the rest of zipper in place being careful to line up rows on both sides. Open zipper up. With WS facing and sewing thread, handsew zipper in place using backstitch (see Glossary). Make sure needle does not go all the way through stitches. At the top of zipper, fold the zipper fabric diagonally and tuck between zipper and crochet fabric. Finish attaching zipper.

Lily
LEG WARMERS

DESIGNED BY JANET BRANI

The dense, stretchy fabric of single crochet rib is perfect for hugging baby legs, so working this project side to side is worth the extra effort of changing colors along each row. Working side to side also makes it easy to custom-fit to little legs, which tend to defy "standard" sizing categories!

FINISHED SIZE

Instructions are written for size 3–12 months. Changes for size 12–24 months are in parentheses. Leg warmers will stretch to fit multiple sizes.

Length: 7½ (9¾)" (19 [25] cm), unstretched.

Circumference at top: 5¾ (7)" (14.5 [18] cm), unstretched.

Circumference at ankle: 4 (5)" (10 [12.5] cm), unstretched.

Shown in size 12–24 months.

YARN

Sportweight (#2 Fine).

Shown here: Schmutzerella Yarns Morphing Mini Skeins (80% superwash merino, 20% nylon; 480 yd [440 m]/4¼ oz [120 g]): The Ghost of Colonel Mustard, 1 package (6 gradient mini skeins of about 80 yd [73 m] per skein). See notes under Yarn Management.

HOOK

Size D/3 (3.25 mm). Adjust hook size if necessary to obtain correct gauge.

NOTIONS

Yarn bobbins (optional); stitch markers; yarn needle.

GAUGE

20 sts and 27 rows = 4" (10 cm) in patt st (sc rib in back loop only). (See instructions for gauge swatch below.)

NOTES

Leg warmers are worked flat, side to side, and each stripe is 6 (8) stitches wide worked in intarsia crochet.

Ribbing at top and bottom is achieved by changing from single crochet to slip stitch as indicated.

All stitches are worked in the back loop only.

All color changes are completed by pulling the new color through to finish the last stitch of the previous color, and the dropped color strand is then crossed over to the front of the work. The stitch worked for the color change is always a single crochet, even when transitioning to or from slip stitch in the ribbing pattern.

GAUGE SWATCH

Row 1: Ch 25, sc in 2nd ch from hook and in each ch across, turn—24 sc.

Row 2: Ch 1, sc blo across, turn.

Rows 3–30: Rep Row 2.

YARN MANAGEMENT

Where the gradient skeins are numbered 1–6 (lightest to darkest), letter your colors as follows: #1 is A, #4 is B, #2 is C, #5 is D, #3 is E, #6 is F.

If using yarn bobbins, wind about 15 (20) yards of each color onto bobbins before beginning.

To prevent tangling of bobbins or yarn balls, begin each row with yarns on your left and move each dropped color to your right as you work across the row.

Leg Warmer (make 2)

With A, ch 37 (49).

Row 1: (RS) Sl st in 2nd ch from hook and in next 4 (6) ch, sc in next ch, *changing to B [see notes on color change], sc in next 6 (8) ch; rep from * with C, D, E, and F across—36 (48) sts, turn.

Row 2: Ch 1, sc 6 (8), sc across, changing color to maintain stripe pattern with colors E, D, C, B, with A, sc 1, sl st 5 (7), turn.

Row 3: Ch 1, sl st 5 (7), sc 1, sc across maintaining stripe pattern with B, C, D, E, with F, sc 1, sl st 5 (7), turn.

Row 4: Ch 1, sl st 5 (7), sc 1, sc across maintaining stripe pattern with E, D, C, B, with A, sc 1, sl st 5 (7), turn.

Row 5: Ch 1, sl st 5 (7), sc 1, sc across maintaining stripe pattern with B, C, D, E, F, turn.

Rows 6–36 (6–44): Rep Rows 2–5 seven (nine) times, rep Rows 2–4 once, do not fasten off, ch 1, turn.

Note: Add or subtract rows, in multiples of 4, to custom fit to the intended recipient.

Finishing

Note: Leg warmer is seamed by slip-stitching tog with RS facing in, changing color across the row to maintain stripe pattern. By working under all lps of beg ch on colors B–F, there is no "show through" of beg chain (color A) on RS.

Fold up (RS facing in) where working yarn is at right, insert hook under unworked lps of beg ch and across in blo of last row, sl st 8, continue to join with sl st across working under *all* lps of beg ch (this is achieved by inserting hook *between* the sts) changing color so join sts match the stripe.

Fasten off. Weave in ends.

Oliver

CABLED EARFLAP HAT

DESIGNED BY A LA SASCHA

The flaps on this sweet hat will keep little ears cozy and warm when it's chilly outside. The versatile design is also equally suitable for both boys and girls. Plus, trying out crochet cables is not so scary when worked in a pint-size design like this.

FINISHED SIZE
Instructions are written for size Newborn–6 months. Changes for 6–12 months and 12–18 months are in parentheses.
Circumference: 12½ (14½, 16½)" (31.5 [37, 42] cm).
Length: 4¾ (6, 7)" (12 [15, 18] cm).
Shown in size 12–18 months.

YARN
Fingering weight (#1 Super Fine).
Shown here: Spud & Chloë Fine (80% superwash wool, 20% silk; 248 yd [227 m]/2¼ oz [65 g]): #7804 cricket, 1 skein.

HOOK
Size G/6 (4 mm). Adjust hook size if necessary to obtain correct gauge.

NOTIONS
Yarn needle; stitch marker (m); 2" (5 cm) pom-pom maker (optional).

GAUGE
6 dc and 7 rows = 1" (2.5 cm).

NOTES
Starting chains do not count as a stitch for entire pattern.

The 6-st cable is worked for size Newborn–6 months, and the 8-st cable is worked for sizes 6–12 (18–24) months.

Hat

Rnd 1: Make an adjustable ring (see Glossary). Ch 2 (does not count as st throughout), 15 dc in ring, join with sl st in first dc—15 sts.

Rnd 2: Ch 2, (dc, FPdc [see Glossary]) in same st as joining, (dc, FPdc) in each dc around, join with sl st in first dc—30 sts.

Rnd 3: Ch 2, *2 dc in next st, FPdc in next st; rep from * around, join with sl st in first dc—45 sts.

Rnd 4: Ch 2, *2 dc in next st, FPdc in next 2 sts; rep from * around, join with sl st in first dc—60 sts.

Size 0-6 Months only

Rnd 5: (cable) Ch 2, *dc in next 2 sts, (sk 3 sts, FPtr [see Glossary] in next 3 sts, FPtr in each of 3 skipped sts behind 3 FPtr group—*cable made*), dc in next 2 sts, FPdc in next 2 sts; rep from * 4 more times, join with sl st in first dc—60 sts.

Rnds 6 and 7: Ch 2, *dc in next 2 sts, FPdc in next 6 sts, dc in next 2 sts, FPdc in next 2 sts; rep from * around, join with sl st in first dc.

Rnds 8-15: Rep Rnds 5-7, ending with a Rnd 6.

Rnd 16: (earflap) Ch 2, *dc in next 11 sts, turn for first earflap, ch 2, dc2tog (see Glossary), dc in next 7 sts, dc2tog, turn, ch 2, dc2tog, dc in next 5 sts, dc2tog, 5 sc evenly along left side of earflap, sc in next 15 sts along edge, ch 1; rep from * once more for second earflap, ending rep with sc in last 23 sts, do not join. Place marker (pm) in first st for beg of rnd.

Rnd 17: *5 sc evenly along right side of first earflap, sc in each st around to next earflap; rep from * once more, join with sl st in first st. Fasten off.

Size 6–12 Months only
Rnd 5: Ch 2, *2 dc in next st, FPdc in next 3 sts; rep from * around, join with sl st in first dc—75 sts.

Rnd 6: (cable) Ch 2, *dc in next 2 sts, (sk 4 sts, FPtr in next 4 sts, FPtr in 4 skipped sts behind 4 FPtr group—cable made), dc in next 2 sts, FPdc in next 3 sts; rep from * 4 more times, join with sl st in first dc.

Rnds 7 and 8: Ch 2, *dc in next 2 sts, FPdc in next 8 sts, dc in next 2 sts, FPdc in next 3 sts; rep from * to * around, join with sl st in first dc.

Rnds 9–20: Rep Rnds 6–8.

Rnd 21: Ch 2, * dc in next 15 sts, turn for first earflap, ch 2, dc2tog, dc in next 11 sts, dc2tog, turn, ch 2, dc2tog, dc in next 9 sts, dc2tog, 5 sc evenly along left side of earflap, sc in next 19 sts along edge, ch 1; rep from * once more for second earflap, ending rep with sc in last 26 sts, do not join. Pm in first st for beg of rnd.

Rnd 22: *5 sc evenly along right side of first earflap, sc in each st around to next earflap; rep from * once more, join with sl st in first sc. Fasten off.

Size 12–18 Months only
Rnd 5: Ch 2, *2 dc in next st, FPdc in next 3 sts; rep from * around, join with sl st in first dc—75 sts.

Rnd 6: Ch 2, *2 dc in next st, dc in next st, FPdc in next 3 sts, 2 dc in next st, FPdc in next 3 sts, 2 dc in next st, dc in next st, FPdc in next 4 sts; rep from * around, join with sl st in first dc—90 sts.

Rnd 7: (cable) Ch 2, *dc in next 3 sts, sk 4 sts, FPtr in next 4 sts, FPtr in each of 4 skipped sts behind 4 FPtr just made, dc in next 3 sts, FPdc in next 4 sts; rep from * around, join with sl st in first dc.

Rnds 8 and 9: Ch 2, *dc in next 3 sts, FPdc in next 8 sts, dc in next 3 sts, FPdc in next 4 sts; rep from * around, sl st in first dc—90 sts.

Rnds 10–23: Rep Rnds 7–9, ending with a Rnd 8.

Rnd 24: Ch 2, *dc in next 19 sts, turn for first earflap, ch 2, dc2tog, dc in next 15 sts, dc2tog, turn, ch 2, dc2tog, dc in next 13 sts, dc2tog, 5 sc evenly along left side of earflap, sc in next 22 sts, ch 1; rep from * once more for second earflap, end rep with sc in last 30 sts, do not join. Pm in first st for beg of rnd.

Rnd 25: *5 sc evenly along right side of first earflap, sc in each st around to next earflap; rep from * once more, join with sl st in first sc. Fasten off.

Finishing
Weave in ends.

Pom-pom (optional): Make pom-pom (see Glossary) about 2" (5 cm) in diameter. Sew to top of hat.

Claire

DRESS

DESIGNED BY KATHY MERRICK

This is a simple, modern dress with a bit of colorwork that's fun and easy. It's not too long and not too short. It's not too snug and not too flowy. It's not too simple and not too fussy. In fact, it's just right for a special little girl.

FINISHED SIZE
Instructions are written for size 12 months. Changes for 18 months and 24 months are in parentheses.

Chest circumference: 19 (20½, 22)" (48.5 [52, 56] cm).

Length: 16¾ (17¾, 18¾)" (42.5 [45, 47.5] cm).

Shown in size 18 months.

YARN
Fingering weight (#1 Super Fine).

Shown here: Madelinetosh Tosh Sock (100% merino; 395 yd [361 m]/3½ oz [100 g]): amber trinket (MC) and mica (CC), 1 skein each.

HOOK
Size F/5 (3.75 mm). Adjust hook size if necessary to obtain correct gauge.

NOTIONS
Two ⅜" (9.5 mm) buttons; yarn needle.

GAUGE
22 sts and 16 rows = 4" (10 cm) in hdc. Row gauge is important for chart.

NOTES
Dress is worked entirely in hdc using intarsia method. When changing colors, work last lp of old color in new color.

Carry yarn not in use across back of work, catching yarn every 4 sts. Work decreases as hdc2tog (see Glossary).

Follow chart for color placement beginning with Row 3 to end of chart. For front, X is color MC. For back, X is color CC.

STITCH GUIDE

Baseball Stitch: With RS of fabrics tog, *insert needle into RS of one piece of fabric, close to the edge between the two facing sides, so it comes out the WS. Loop the needle around toward where the two pieces come tog, and again, insert needle into RS of opposite piece of fabric so it comes out the WS; rep from * along edge.

Back

Note: Work entire intarsia chart beg with Row 3.

With MC, ch 61 (65, 69).

Row 1: Skip 2 ch (counts as hdc), hdc in 3rd ch from hook and in each ch across—60 (64, 68) sts.

Row 2: Ch 2 (counts as hdc throughout), hdc in each st across.

Rows 3–6: Ch 2, beg chart in MC and adding CC.

Row 7: (dec) Ch 2, hdc2tog (see Glossary), work chart in hdc to last 3 sts, hdc2tog, hdc in last st—58 (62, 66) sts.

Rows 8–12: Ch 2, work even in chart in hdc.

Row 13: Ch 2, hdc2tog, work chart in hdc to last 3 sts, hdc2tog, hdc in last st—56 (60, 64) sts.

Rows 14–16 (14–18, 14–18): Ch 2, work even in chart in hdc.

Row 17 (19, 19): Ch 2, hdc2tog, work chart in hdc to last 3 sts, hdc2tog, hdc in last st—54 (58, 62) sts.

Rows 18–20 (20–22, 20–22): Work even in chart in hdc.

Row 21 (23, 23): Ch 2, hdc2tog, work chart in hdc to last 3 sts, hdc2tog, hdc in last st—52 (56, 60) sts.

Rows 22–52 (24–54, 24–56): Ch 2, work even in chart in hdc until back measures 13 (13½, 14)" (33 [34.5, 35.5] cm).

SHAPE ARMHOLES

Row 53 (55, 57): Sl st across first 4 sts, ch 2, work chart in hdc to last 4 sts, turn—44 (48, 52) sts.

Row 54 (56, 58): Ch 2, [hdc2tog] twice, work chart in hdc to last 5 sts, [hdc2tog] twice, hdc in last st—40 (44, 48) sts.

Row 55 (57, 59): Ch 2, hdc2tog, work chart in hdc to last 3 sts, hdc2tog, hdc in last st—38 (42, 46) sts.

Row 56 (58, 60): Ch 2, work even in chart in hdc.

Row 57 (59, 61): Ch 2, hdc2tog, work chart in hdc to last 3 sts, hdc2tog, hdc in last st—36 (40, 44) sts.

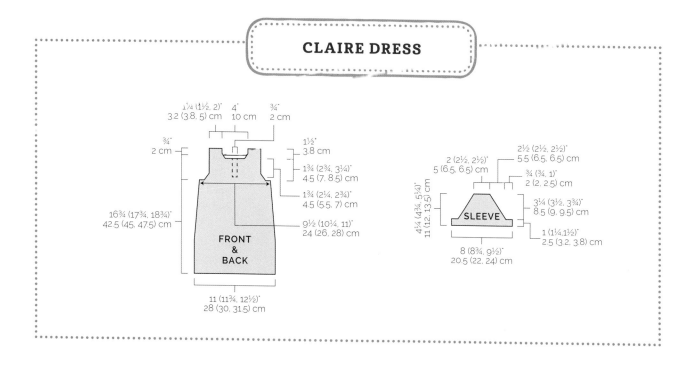

Rows 58–64 (60–68, 62–72): Ch 2, work even in chart in hdc until arm-hole measures 3 (3½, 4)" (7.5 [9, 10] cm).

SHAPE NECK RIGHT SIDE

Row 65 (69, 73): Ch 2, work chart in hdc in next 7 (9, 11) sts—8 (10, 12) sts, turn.

Row 66 (70, 74): Ch 2, hdc2tog, work chart in hdc in next 5 (7, 9) hdc—7 (9, 11) sts, turn.

Row 67 (71, 75): Ch 2, work even in chart in hdc. Fasten off.

SHAPE NECK LEFT SIDE

Skip center 20 sts, attach yarn in next st.

Row 65 (69, 73): Ch 2, work chart in hdc in next 7 (9, 11) sts—8 (10, 12) sts, turn.

Row 66 (70, 74): Ch 2, work chart in hdc in next 4 (6, 8) sts, hdc2tog, hdc in last st—7 (9, 11) sts.

Row 67 (71, 75): Ch 2, work even in chart in hdc. Fasten off.

Front

Work as for back and armhole shaping, reversing MC and CC, through Row 54 (56, 58) following chart, turn.

SHAPE NECK LEFT SIDE

Row 55 (57, 59): Ch 2, hdc2tog, hdc in next 15 (17, 19) sts, hdc blo in next 4 sts (leaving front lps to be worked on right side for tab)—21 (23, 25) sts, turn.

Row 56 (58, 60): Ch 2, work even in chart, turn.

Row 57 (59, 61): Ch 2, hdc2tog, hdc in next 18 (20, 22) sts—20 (22, 24) sts, turn.

Rows 58–61 (60–65, 62–69): Ch 2, work even in chart for 4 (6, 8) rows, turn.

Row 62 (66, 70): Sl st across first 10 (10, 10) sts, hdc to end—10 (12, 14) sts, turn.

Row 63 (67, 71): Ch 2, hdc in next 6 (8, 10) sts, hdc2tog, hdc in last st—9 (11, 13) sts, turn.

Row 64 (68, 72): Ch 2, hdc2tog, hdc in next 6 (8, 10) sts—8 (10, 12) sts. turn.

Row 65 (69, 73): Ch 2, hdc in next 4 (6, 8) sts, hdc2tog, hdc in last st—7 (9, 11) sts, turn.

Rows 66 and 67 (70 and 71, 74 and 75): Ch 2, work 2 rows even in chart. Fasten off.

SHAPE NECK RIGHT SIDE

Row 55 (57, 59): With RS facing, join yarn in first hdc that was worked in the back lp, hdc flo in each of next 4

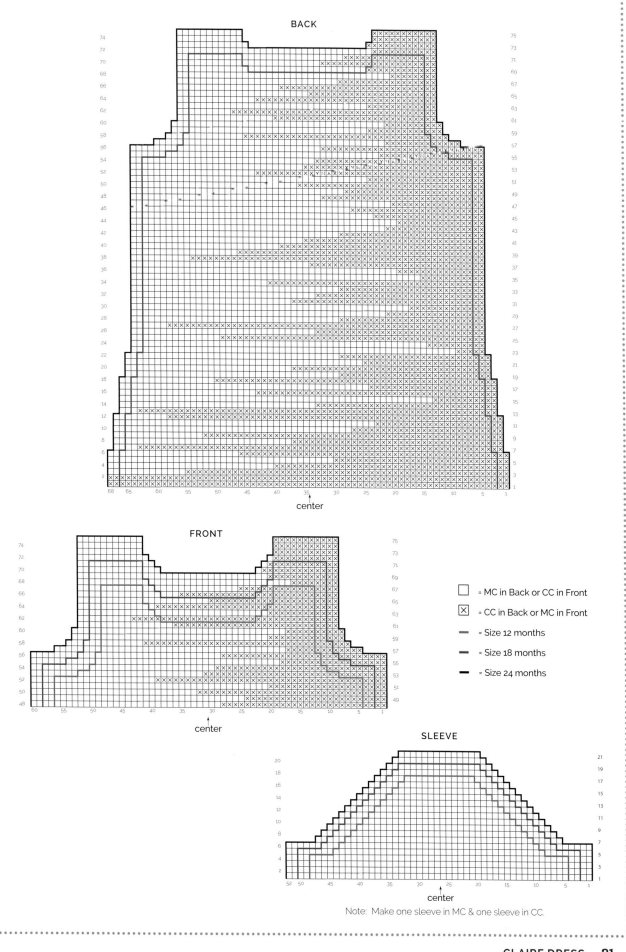

BACK

FRONT

SLEEVE

center

center

center

= MC in Back or CC in Front

= CC in Back or MC in Front

= Size 12 months

= Size 18 months

= Size 24 months

Note: Make one sleeve in MC & one sleeve in CC.

hdc blo of left side (this beg tab over-lap), hdc in next 15 (17, 19) sts, hdc2tog, hdc—21 (23, 25) sts, turn.

Row 56 (58, 60): (buttonhole) Ch 2, hdc to last 3 sts, ch 2, sk 2 hdc, hdc in last st, turn.

Row 57 (59, 61): Ch 2, 2 hdc in ch-2 sp, hdc in each st across to last 3 sts, hdc-2tog, hdc in last st—20 (22, 24) sts.

Rows 58 and 59 (60–63, 62–67): Ch 2, work even in chart for 2 (4, 6) rows, turn.

Row 60 (64, 68): (buttonhole) Ch 2, hdc in each st to last 3 sts, ch 2, sk 2 hdc, hdc in last st, turn.

Row 61 (65, 69): Ch 2, 2 hdc in ch-2 sp, hdc in each st across.

Row 62 (66, 70): Ch 2, hdc in next 9 (11, 13) sts, leave rem sts unworked—10 (12, 14) sts, turn.

Row 63 (67, 71): Ch 2, hdc2tog, hdc in next 7 (9, 11) sts—9 (11, 13) sts, turn.

Row 64 (68, 72): Ch 2, hdc in next 5 (7, 9) sts, hdc2tog, hdc in last st—8 (10, 12) sts, turn.

Row 65 (69, 73): Ch 2, hdc2tog, hdc in next 5 (7, 9) sts, hdc in last st—7 (9, 11) sts, turn.

Rows 66 and 67 (70 and 71, 74 and 75): Ch 2, work 2 rows even in chart. Fasten off.

Sleeve (make 1 color MC and 1 color CC)

Ch 45 (49, 53).

Row 1: Hdc in 3rd ch from hook and in each ch across—44 (48, 52) sts.

Rows 2–4 (2–5, 2–6): Ch 2, hdc in each st across.

SHAPE SLEEVE CAP

Row 5 (6, 7): Sl st across 4 (4, 5) hdc, hdc to last 4 (4, 5) hdc, leave rem sts unworked—36 (40, 42) sts, turn.

Row 6 (7, 8): (dec) Ch 2, hdc2tog, hdc in each st to last 3 sts, hdc2tog, hdc in last st—34 (38, 40) sts, turn.

Rows 7–17 (8–19, 9–21): Rep dec row 11 (12, 13) more times—12 (14, 14) sts. Fasten off.

Finishing

Block pieces to finished measurements. Using baseball stitch (see Stitch Guide) for sewing and to keep seams flat, sew shoulders tog. Sew sleeves to armholes, fitting sleeve cap across last row and down sleeve side. Sew armhole and side seams. Press seams flat.

Sew buttons opposite buttonholes.

Parker

PANTS

DESIGNED BY SHARON ZIENTARA

These pants are a baby's version of long johns. The linen-stitch fabric is cozy and warm, and the yarn has just the right amount of stretch to allow baby to be active and agile.

FINISHED SIZE

Instructions are written for size Newborn–3 months. Changes for 3–6 months, 6–12 months, 12–18 months, 18–24 months, and 2–3 years are in parentheses.

Waist circumference: 17¾ (19, 20, 21, 21¾, 23)" (45 [48.5, 51, 53.5, 55, 58.5] cm).

Length: 17 (18¾, 19½, 21¼, 22, 24¾)" (43 [47.5, 49.5, 54, 56, 63] cm).

Shown in size 6–12 months.

YARN

Fingering weight (#1 Super Fine).

Shown here: Cascade Yarns Heritage Sock (75% merino, 25% nylon; 437 yd [400 m]/3½ oz [100 g]): #5610 camel (MC) and #5642 blood orange (CC), 1 skein each.

HOOK

Size E/4 (3.5 mm). Adjust hook size if necessary to obtain correct gauge.

NOTIONS

Stitch markers (m); yarn needle.

GAUGE

26 sts and 23 rows = 4" (10 cm) in pattern.

NOTES

Pants are crocheted from waist down. Legs are each worked separately, and ribbing is picked up for waistband after pants are completed.

Instructions for an optional I-cord drawstring are included, although not shown in the sample pictured.

For gauge swatch, ch a multiple of 2 sts, join with sl st in beg ch. Work Rnds 1–4 of pants instructions, then rep Rnds 3 and 4 for patt.

Decreases (sc2tog) at inseam are worked over 3 sts (see Stitch Guide). Choose the decrease that best fits the patt in the row being worked.

Sc2tog over 3 sts (ch-1 sp, sc, ch-1 sp): Sc2tog over next 2 ch-sps, skipping center sc—2 sts decreased.

Sc2tog over 3 sts (sc, ch-1 sp, sc): Sc2tog over next 2 sc, skipping center ch-sp—2 sts decreased.

Pants

With MC, ch 116 (124, 130, 136, 142, 150), join with sl st to first ch being careful not to twist ch.

Rnd 1: Ch 2 (counts as ch 1 and ch-1 sp throughout), sk same ch as joining, *sc in next ch, ch 1, sk next ch; rep from * around, end sc in last ch, join with sl st in beg ch-2—116 (124, 130, 136, 142, 150) sts, do not turn.

Rnd 2: Ch 1, sc in first ch-sp, *ch 1, sk next sc, sc in next ch sp; rep from * around, end ch 1, sk last sc, join with sl st in first sc, do not turn, drop MC (do not fasten off) and join CC with sl st in same sp as joining.

Rnd 3: With CC, ch 2, sk first sc, *sc in next ch-sp, ch 1, sk next sc; rep from * around, end sc in last ch-sp, join with sl st in beg ch-1, do not turn, drop CC.

Rnd 4: With MC, ch 1, sc in first ch-sp, *ch 1, sk next sc, sc in next ch-sp; rep from * around, end ch 1, sk last sc, join with sl st in first sc, do not turn, drop MC.

Rep Rnds 3 and 4 until 36 (40, 44, 48, 52, 58) rows have been worked, drop MC, do not fasten off.

DIVIDE FOR LEGS

Pm in 28th (30th, 31st, 33rd, 34th, 35th) sts, and 32nd (34th, 36th, 37th, 39th, 41st) sts, and the 86th (92nd, 96th, 101st, 105th, 111th) and 90th (96th, 101st, 105th, 110th, 116th) sts to mark inseam.

FIRST LEG

Rnd 37 (41, 45, 49, 53, 59): (divide for legs) With CC, ch 2, sk first sc, *sc in next ch-sp, ch 1, sk next sc; rep from * to first marked st, sk first marked st and turn to face 90th (96th, 101st, 105th, 110th, 116th) marked st, cont in patt beg in marked st and around, join with sl st in beg ch-2—54 (58, 60, 64, 66, 70) sts, drop CC, do not turn.

Rnd 38 (42, 46, 50, 54, 60): With MC, ch 1, sc in first ch-sp, *ch 1, sk next sc, sc in next ch-sp; rep from * around, end with ch 1, sk last sc, join with sl st in first sc, drop MC, do not turn.

Rnd 39 (43, 47, 51, 55, 61): (dec) With CC, ch 2, sk first sc, sc in next ch-sp, *ch 1, sk next sc, sc in next ch-sp; rep from * to center 3 sts, sc2tog (see Glossary), work in patt around, join with sl st in beg ch-2—52 (56, 58, 62, 64, 68) sts, drop CC, do not turn.

Rnd 40 (44, 48, 52, 56, 62): With MC, rep Rnd 38 (42, 46, 50, 54, 60), drop MC, do not turn.

Rnd 41 (45, 49, 53, 57, 63): With CC, ch 2, work even in patt around, join with sl st to beg ch-2, drop CC, do not turn.

Rnd 42 (46, 50, 54, 58, 64): With MC, rep Rnd 38 (42, 46, 50, 54, 60), drop MC, do not turn.

Rnd 43 (47, 51, 55, 59, 65): (dec) With CC, rep Rnd 39 (43, 47, 51, 55, 61), drop CC, do not turn.

Rnds 44–59 (48–63, 52–79, 56–71, 60–91, 66–109): Cont in color sequence and rep Rnds 40–43 (44–47, 48–51, 52–55, 56–59, 62–65) decreasing every 4th row 4 (4, 7, 4, 8, 11) more times—42 (46, 42, 52, 46, 44) sts.

Rnds 60 and 61 (64 and 65, 80 and 81, 72 and 73, 92 and 93, 110 and 111): Work 2 rows even in pattt, drop CC in last rnd.

Rnd 62 (66, 82, 74, 94, 112): (dec) With MC, ch 1, sc in first ch-sp, *ch 1, sk next ch-sp, sc in next ch-sp: rep from * to center 3 sts, sc2tog (see Glossary), work in patt around, join with sl st in first sc—40 (44, 40, 50, 44, 42) sts, do not turn.

Rnds 63–89 (67–105, 83–103, 75–113, 95–121, 113–133): Cont in color sequence and rep Rnds 60–62 (64–66, 80–82, 72–74, 92–94, 110–112) decreasing every 3rd row 9 (13, 7, 13, 9, 7) more times—22 (22, 26, 24, 26, 28) sts.

Rnds 90–92 (106–108, 104–106, 114–116, 122–124, 134–136): Work 3 rows even in patt. Do not fasten off MC, turn pant leg 90 degrees to work bottom hem ribbing.

Bottom Cuff Ribbing

Row 1: With MC, ch 5, sc blo in 2nd ch from hook and in each ch across, sl st in next 2 sts on bottom edge of pant—4 sts, turn.

Row 2: Sc blo in each st across, turn.

Row 3: Ch 1 (tightly to keep a neat edge to ribbing), sc blo in first and each st across, sl st in next 2 sts on bottom edge of pant, turn.

Rep last 2 rows around entire edge of pant leg. Fasten off.

SECOND LEG
Sizes 0–3 (3–6, 6–12) Months only
Rnd 37 (41, 45): Join CC with a sl st in marked 32nd (34th, 36th) st, ch 1, sc in same st as joining, ch 1, sk next sc, *sc in next ch-sp, ch 1, sk next sc; rep from * to next marker, sk marker, join with sl st in first sc—54 (58, 60) sts, drop CC, join MC with sl st in same st as joining, do not turn.

Rnd 38 (42, 46): With MC, ch 2, sk first sc, *sc in next ch-sp, ch 1, sk next ch-sp, sc in next st; rep from * around, join with sl st in beg ch-2, drop MC, do not turn.

Rnd 39 (43, 47): (dec) With CC, ch 1, sc2tog (see Glossary), work in patt around, join with sl st in first sc—52 (56, 58) sts, drop CC, do not turn.

Rnd 40 (44, 48): With MC, ch 2, work even in patt around, join with sl st in beg ch-2, drop MC, do not turn.

Rnd 41 (45, 49): With CC, ch 1, work even in patt around, join with sl st in first sc, drop CC, do not turn.

Rnd 42 (46, 50): With MC, work even in patt around, join with sl st in beg ch-2, drop MC, do not turn.

Rnd 43 (47, 51): (dec) With CC, ch 1, sc2tog, work in patt around, join with sl st in first sc—50 (54, 56) sts, drop MC, do not turn.

Rnds 44–59 (48–63, 52–79): Cont in color sequence and rep Rnds 40–43 (44–47, 48–51) decreasing every

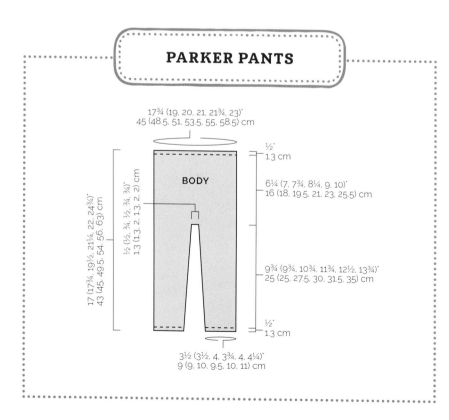

PARKER PANTS

BODY

17¾ (19, 20, 21, 21¾, 23)"
45 (48.5, 51, 53.5, 55, 58.5) cm

½"
1.3 cm

6¼ (7, 7¾, 8¼, 9, 10)"
16 (18, 19.5, 21, 23, 25.5) cm

9¾ (9¾, 10¾, 11¾, 12½, 13¾)"
25 (25, 27.5, 30, 31.5, 35) cm

½"
1.3 cm

17 (17¾, 19½, 21¼, 22, 24¾)"
43 (45, 49.5, 54, 56, 63) cm

½ (½, ¾, ½, ¾, ¾)"
1.3 (1.3, 2, 1.3, 2, 2) cm

3½ (3½, 4, 3¾, 4, 4¼)"
9 (9, 10, 9.5, 10, 11) cm

4th row 4 (4, 7) more times—42 (46, 42) sts.

Rnds 60 and 61 (64 and 65, 80 and 81): Work 2 rows even in patt, drop CC in last rnd.

Rnd 62 (66, 82): (dec) With MC, ch 1, sc in first ch-sp, *ch 1, sk next ch-sp, sc in next ch-sp; rep from * to center 3 sts, sc2tog (see Glossary), work in patt around, join with sl st in first sc—40 (40, 40) sts, do not turn.

Rnds 63–89 (67–93, 83–103): Cont in color sequence and rep Rnds 60–62 (64–66, 80–82) decreasing every 3rd row 9 (9, 7) more times—22 (22, 26) sts.

Rnds 90–92 (94–96, 104–106): Work 3 rows even in patt. Do not fasten off MC.

Turn pant leg 90 degrees to work bottom cuff ribbing as for first leg. Fasten off.

Sizes 12–18 Months (18–24 Months, 2–3 Years) only

Rnd 49 (53, 59): Join CC with a sl st in marked 37th (39th, 41st) st, ch 2, sk first sc, sc in next ch-sp, *ch 1, sk next sc, sc in next ch-1 sp; rep from * to next marker, sk marker, join with sl st in beg ch-2—64 (66, 70) sts, drop CC, join MC with sl st in same st as joining, do not turn.

Rnd 50 (54, 60): With MC, ch 1, sc in 1st ch-sp, ch 1, sk next ch-sp, *sc in next st, ch 1, sk next ch-sp; rep from * around, join with sl st in first sc, drop MC, do not turn.

Rnd 51 (55, 61): (dec) With CC, ch 1, sc2tog (see Glossary), work in patt around, join with sl st in first sc—62 (64, 68) sts, drop CC, do not turn.

Rnd 52 (56, 62): With MC, work even in patt around, drop MC, do not turn.

Rnd 53 (57, 63): With CC, work even in patt around, drop CC, do not turn.

Rnd 54 (58, 64): With MC, work even in patt around, drop MC, do not turn.

Rnd 55 (59, 65): (dec) With CC, ch 1, sc2tog, work in patt around, join with sl st in first sc—60 (62, 66) sts, drop CC, do not turn.

Rnds 56–71 (60–91, 66–109): Cont in color sequence and rep Rnds 52–55 (56–59, 62–65) decreasing every 4th row 4 (8, 11) more times—52 (46, 44) sts.

Rnds 72 and 73 (92 and 93, 110 and 111): Work 2 rows even in patt, drop CC in last rnd.

Rnd 74 (94, 112): (dec) With MC, ch 1, sc2tog, work in patt around, join with sl st in first sc—50 (44, 42) sts, do not turn.

Rnds 75–113 (95–121, 113–133): Cont in color sequence and rep Rnds 72–74 (92–94, 110–112) decreasing every 3rd row 13 (9, 7) more times—24 (26, 28) sts.

Rnds 114–116 (122–124, 134–136): Work 3 rows even in pattern. Do not fasten off MC.

Turn pant leg 90 degrees to work bottom cuff ribbing as for first leg.

WAISTBAND
Join MC in any st at waist edge.

Row 1: Ch 5, sc blo in 2nd ch from hook and in each ch across, sl st in next 2 sts on waist edge—4 sts, turn.

Row 2: Sc blo in each st across, turn.

Row 3: Ch 1 (tightly to keep a neat edge to ribbing), sc blo in each st across, sl st in next 2 sts on waistband, turn.

Rep Rows 2 and 3 around entire waist edge. Fasten off.

Drawstring (I-Cord; optional)
With MC, ch 3, insert hook in 2nd ch from hook, yo and pull up a lp, insert hook in next ch, yo and pull up a lp (3 lps on hook).

Row 1: Remove hook from first 2 lps pinching lps bet fingers with non-hook hand so they do not become loose. Yo and draw through remaining lp on hook. Insert hook into first dropped lp, yo and pull up a lp (2 lps on hook), insert hook into second dropped lp, yo and pull up a lp (3 lps remaining on hook).

Rep Row 1 for 23¾ [25, 26, 27, 28¾, 29]") [60.5 (63.5, 66, 68.5, 73, 73,5) cm]. Fasten off and draw tail end through all 3 lps on hook.

Finishing
Weave in ends. Sew seams of waist and cuff ribbings. Sew crotch seam between legs. Block if desired.

Weave drawstring into WS and out to RS between waist edge and ribbing beg at center front, around to back, and ending at back at center front.

Cameron
BLANKET

DESIGNED BY CRISTINA MERSHON

A simple, stylish baby blanket is the perfect gift for any mom-to-be, especially when worked in practical washable wool. It's just the right size to tuck around little legs when out in the stroller. You could easily whip up a few at a time to have on hand for last-minute gift giving.

FINISHED SIZE
22½" (57 cm) wide and 21" (53.5 cm) long.

YARN
Worsted weight (#4 Medium).
Shown here: Cascade Yarns 220 Superwash (100% superwash wool; 220 yd [200 m]/3½ oz [100 g]): #910A winter white (A), #1946 silver grey (B), and #900 charcoal (C), 1 skein each.

HOOK
Size D/3 (3.25 mm).

NOTIONS
Stitch markers; yarn needle.

GAUGE
9¼ sts and 10 rows = 2" (5 cm) in patt. Gauge is not critical for this project.

NOTES
The blanket is worked sideways so the ripple effect shows vertically.

After the first row, all stitches are worked in the back loop only.

As colors change constantly, either fasten off and weave ends with every color change or simply hold open lps with stitch markers, carrying yarn up the side of the work.

Blanket

Color Sequence: [A, B, and C] 15 times.

With color A, ch 106, turn.

Row 1: (RS) Sl st in 2nd ch from hook and in each of next 4 ch, *hdc next 5 ch, sl st in next 5 ch; rep from * across to end of row—105 sts, turn.

Row 2: With color A, ch 1, sl st blo in first 5 sl st, *hdc blo in next 5 hdc, sl st blo in next 5 sl st; rep from * across to end of row, turn.

Row 3: Join color B with sl st, ch 2 (does not count as st throughout), hdc blo in next 5 sl st, *sl st blo in next 5 hdc, hdc blo in next 5 sl st; rep from * across to end of row, turn.

Row 4: With color B, ch 2, hdc blo in next 5 hdc, *sl st blo in next 5 sl st, hdc blo in next 5 hdc; rep from * across to end of row, turn.

Row 5: Join color C with sl st, ch 1, sl st blo in first 5 hdc, *hdc blo in next 5 sl st, sl st blo in next 5 hdc; rep from * across to end of row, turn.

Row 6: With color C, ch 1, sl st blo in first 5 sl st, *hdc blo in next 5 hdc, sl st blo in next 5 sl st; rep from * across to end of row, turn.

Rows 7–90: Rep Rows 3–6 continuing in color sequence. Fasten off.

Finishing

Weave in ends. Block if desired.

Zoe the Cat
SLIPPERS

DESIGNED BY BRENDA K. B. ANDERSON

Designer Brenda Anderson's cat, Mr. Kittypants, is round and adorable. When he lies down on the floor, he sometimes tucks his feet under his body, and he looks like he doesn't have any legs. Brenda re-created this effect, which she likes to call a "kitty-cat-loaf," for these darling kitty slippers.

FINISHED SIZE
Instructions are written for size Newborn–3 months. Changes for 3–6 months, 6–12 months, 12–18 months, and 18–24 months are in parentheses.

Length of sole: 3¼ (3½, 3¾, 4¼, 4¾)" (8.5 [9, 9.5, 11, 12] cm).

Shown in size 18–24 months. Slippers stay on feet best if they stretch about ¼" (6 mm) to fit (i.e., if foot measures about ¼" [6 mm] longer than sole of slipper).

YARN
DK weight (#3 Light).

Shown here: Berroco Vintage DK (52% acrylic, 40% wool, 8% nylon; 288 yd [263 m]/3½ oz [100 g]): #2106 smoke, 1 skein.

HOOK
Size D/3 (3.25 mm). Adjust hook size if necessary to obtain correct gauge.

NOTIONS
Stitch markers (m); yarn needle; sewing or quilter's pins; small amount of polyester stuffing to stuff tail; black and light pink embroidery floss and embroidery needle; 2" × 3" (5 × 7.5 cm) piece of light pink felt for inner ear decoration; pink sewing thread and sewing needle for attaching felt to ears.

GAUGE
22 sts and 26 rows = 4" (10 cm) in sc worked in turned rows.

Slipper (make 2)

TOE

Foundation Chain: Ch 7 (6, 7, 9, 9) sts.

Rnd 1: (RS) Beg with 2nd ch from hook and working into the bottom of ch, 2 sc in next st, sc in next 4 (3, 4, 6, 6) sts, 2 sc in the last st. Rotate work 180 degrees (like turning a steering wheel) in order to work in opposite side of foundation ch, 2 sc in next st, sc in next 4 (3, 4, 6, 6) sts, 2 sc in next st, do not join but work in a spiral—16 (14, 16, 20, 20) sts. Use a stitch marker to keep track of the first st of rnd.

Rnd 2: [2 sc in next st, sc in next 6 (5, 6, 8, 8) sts, 2 sc in next st] twice—20 (18, 20, 24, 24) sts.

Rnd 3: [2 sc in next st, sc in next 8 (7, 8, 10, 10) sts, 2 sc in next st] twice—24 (22, 24, 28, 28) sts. Work 1 sc to shift beg of rnd. First st of the next rnd will count as new beg of rnd.

Rnd 4: Sc in each st around—24 (22, 24, 28, 28) sts.

Sizes 3–6 (6–12, 12–18, 18–24) Months only

Rnd 5: [2 Sc in next st, sc in next 9 (10, 12, 12) sts, 2 sc in next st] twice—26 (28, 32, 32) sts.

Rnd 6: Sc around—26 (28, 32, 32) sts. Work 1 sc to shift beg of rnd. First st of next rnd will count as new beg of rnd.

Size 18–24 Months only

Rnd 7: [2 sc in next st, sc in next 14 sts, 2 sc in next st] twice—36 sts.

All Sizes

Rnds 5–11 (7–12, 7–13, 7–15, 8–16): Sc around—24 (26, 28, 32, 36) sts. Place marker in 9th (10th, 11th, 13th, 14th) st of the last rnd.

Fasten off.

SIDES

Row 1: With RS facing, pull up yarn in marked st, ch 1, beg with same st, sc2tog, sc in next 16 (17, 19, 22, 26) sts, sc2tog, leave remaining 4 (5, 5, 6, 6) sts unworked—18 (19, 21, 24, 28) sts.

Row 2: Ch 1, turn (WS now facing), sc2tog, sc in next 14 (15, 17, 20, 24) sts, sc2tog—16 (17, 19, 22, 26) sts.

Sizes 12–18 (18–24) Months only

Row 3: Ch 1, turn (RS now facing) sc2tog, sc in next 18 (22) sts, sc2tog—20 (24) sts.

Size 18–24 Months only

Row 4: Ch 1, turn, sc2tog, sc in next 20 sts, sc2tog—22 sts.

All Sizes

Rows 3–7 (3–8, 3–9, 4–8, 5–10): Ch 1, turn, sc around—16 (17, 19, 20, 22) sts.

Row 8 (9, 10, 9, 11): Ch 1, turn, 2 sc in next st, sc in next 14 (15, 17, 18, 20) sts, 2 sc in next st—18 (19, 21, 22, 24) sts.

Row 9 (10, 11, 10, 12): Ch 1, turn, 2 sc in next st, sc in next 16 (17, 19, 20, 22) sts, 2 sc in next st—20 (21, 23, 24, 26) sts.

Sizes 12–18 (18–24) Months only

Row 11 (13): Ch 1, turn, 2 sc in next st, sc in next 22 (24) sts, 2 sc in next st—26 (28) sts.

All Sizes

Row 10 (11, 12, 12, 14): Ch 1, turn, sc in next 6 (6, 7, 9, 10) sts, sc2tog, sc in next 4 (5, 5, 4, 4) sts, sc2tog, sc in next 6 (6, 7, 9, 10) sts—18 (19, 21, 24, 26) sts.

Row 11 (12, 13, 13, 15): Ch 1, turn, sc in next 6 (6, 7, 9, 10) sts, sc2tog, sc in next 2 (3, 3, 2, 2) sts, sc2tog, sc in next 6 (6, 7, 9, 10) sts—16 (17, 19, 22, 24) sts.

Row 12 (13, 14, 14, 16): Ch 1, turn, sc in next 6 (6, 7, 9, 10) sts, sc2tog, sc in next 0 (1, 1, 0, 0) st(s), sc2tog, sc in next 6 (6, 7, 9, 10) sts—14 (15, 17, 20, 22) sts.

Row 13 (14, 15, 15, 17): Ch 1, turn, sc in next 5 (5, 6, 8, 9) sts, sc2tog, sc in next 0 (1, 1, 0, 0) st(s), sc2tog, sc in next 5 (5, 6, 8, 9) sts—12 (13, 15, 18, 20) sts.

Sizes 12–18 (18–24) Months only

Row 16 (18): Ch 1, turn, sc in next 7 (8) sts, [sc2tog] twice, sc in next 7 (8) sts—16 (18) sts.

All Sizes

Fasten off, leaving a long tail for sewing.

Match up the first and last stitch of the last row worked by folding edge in half. Using yarn tail and yarn needle, whipstitch (see Glossary) the back of heel together. Weave in ends.

EDGING AROUND ANKLE OPENING

Rnd 1: Pull up yarn at ankle opening near center back seam in heel. Ch 1, sc 11 (12, 13, 14, 16) evenly spaced along side of opening, sc 4 (5, 5, 6, 6) in sts across front of ankle opening, sc 11 (12, 13, 14, 16) evenly spaced along other side of ankle opening, ending at center back—26 (29, 31, 34, 38) sc around ankle opening. Do not join.

Rnds 2 and 3: Sc blo around—26 (29, 31, 34, 38) sts.

Note: This edging should make the ankle opening a little bit smaller than it was; it is meant to help keep slippers on feet as well as to provide a nice edge. Opening will stretch a little, but make sure that the opening does not get so small that you cannot put the slippers on.

Fasten off and weave in end.

Tail (make 2)

Rnd 1: Leaving long tail for sewing, make an adjustable ring, 6 sc in ring, pull on beg tail to close ring—6 sc. Do not join.

Rnd 2: [2 sc in next st, sc in next st] 3 times—9 sts.

Next rnds: Sc around until tail measures about 2¾ (3, 3¼, 3½, 4)" (7 [7.5, 8.5, 9, 10] cm) long. Stuff lightly with polyester stuffing as you work. Do not fasten off.

Next rnd: [2 sc in next st, sc in next 2 sts] 3 times—12 sts.

Next rnd: [2 sc in next st, sc in next 3 sts] 3 times—15 sts.

Fasten off, leaving a long tail for sewing.

Using most recent yarn tail and yarn needle, stitch the open end of tail to the center back of the heel of slipper. This should be positioned near the bottom of the slipper; see photos for placement. Gently wrap tail around side of slipper, being careful not to pull too tightly and distort heel of slipper. Make sure that one tail wraps to the left and the other wraps to the right. Pin in place using photos for a placement guide. Use other yarn tail and yarn needle to stitch side of tail to side of slipper. Weave in ends.

Ear (make 4)

Rnd 1: Make an adjustable ring, 6 sc in ring, pull on beg tail to tighten ring—6 sc. Do not join.

Rnd 2: [2 sc in next st, sc in next st] 3 times—9 sts.

Rnd 3: [2 sc in next st, sc in next 2 sts] 3 times—12 sts.

Rnd 4: [2 sc in next st, sc in next 3 sts] 3 times—15 sts.

Sizes 3–6 (6–12) Months only
Rnd 5: [2 sc in next st, sc in next 4 sts] 3 times—18 sts.

Size 12–18 Months only
Rnd 6: [2 sc in next st, sc in next 5 sts] 3 times—21 sts.

Size 18–24 Months only
Rnd 7: Sc around—21 sts.

All Sizes
Fasten off, leaving a long tail for sewing.

Finishing

Block all pieces if needed. Fold ears flat and cut out small triangles of pink felt to line front side of each ear. Using sewing needle and matching thread, whipstitch edges of felt to front of each ear. Pin bottom edge of each ear to slipper using photos as a guide for placement. Bottom edge of each ear should be slightly curved in a C shape. This will help the ear stand upright as well as give it shape. Using yarn tails and yarn needle, stitch bottom of ears to slipper. Weave in all yarn ends. Using pink embroidery floss and needle, embroider a triangle on toe of slipper for a nose using a satin stitch (see Glossary). Using black embroidery floss make 2 large French knots (see Glossary) for eyes, outline the bottom sides of the nose triangle, embroider the mouth curves, and make whiskers on each cheek.

Liam

ZIPPERED PULLOVER

DESIGNED BY ROBYN CHACHULA

Tunisian stitches produce some of the most interesting fabrics, all based on where and how you insert your hook. The key to the stitch pattern used in this versatile pullover is the twisted simple stitch. By inserting your hook in the opposite direction of a regular simple stitch, you get a beautiful knit-looking V without any extra weight that a knit stitch can sometimes add.

FINISHED SIZE

Instructions are written for size Newborn–6 months. Changes for 6–12 months, 12–18 months, and 18–24 months are in parentheses.

Chest circumference: 22½ (24½, 26½, 29)" (57 [62, 67.5, 73.5] cm).

Shown in size 12–18 months.

YARN

Sportweight (#2 Fine).

Shown here: O-wool O-wash Sport (100% machine-washable certified organic merino; 306 yd [280 m]/3½ oz [100 g]): cuckoo flower, 2 hanks.

HOOK

Size J/10 (6 mm) Tunisian hook. Adjust hook size if necessary to obtain correct gauge.

NOTIONS

Yarn needle; 7" (18 cm) nonseparating zipper; matching sewing thread; sewing pins.

GAUGE

15 sts and 12¾ rows = 4" (10 cm) in stitch pattern.

NOTE

Horizontal lines are created using slip-stitch embroidery along the rows of Tunisian Simple Stitch after the front and back panels are completed.

TUNISIAN SIMPLE STITCH (TSS)

Tss forward pass (FwP): *Insert hook from right to left behind front vertical bar **(Figure 1)**, yo and pull up lp **(Figure 2)**, leave lp on hook; repeat from * to last vertical bar at edge, pick up front and back lps of last bar to create firm edge; return pass.

Tss return pass (RetP): Work off lps as normal. Yo and draw through first lp on hook, *yo and draw through 2 lps on hook **(Figure 3)**; repeat from * to end, ending with 1 lp on hook.

TUNISIAN PURL STITCH (TPS)

Tps forward pass (FwP): Bring yarn to the front of the work, *Insert hook from right to left behind front vertical bar, yo and pull up lp **(Figure 4),** leave lp on hook; repeat from * to last vertical bar at edge, pick up front and back lps of last bar to create firm edge; return pass.

Tps return pass (RetP): Work as for Tss RetP.

TUNISIAN KNIT STITCH (TKS)

Tks forward pass (Fwp): Skip first vertical bars, with yarn in back, *insert hook between next vertical bars under horizontal strands **(Figure 5)**, yo and pull up lp, leave lp on hook; repeat from * to end, ending with 1 lp on hook; return pass.

Tks return pass (RetP): Yo and draw lp through first lp on hook, *yo and draw through 2 lps on hook: repeat from * across **(Figure 6)**, ending with 1 lp on hook.

TWISTED SIMPLE STITCH (TWTSS)

TwTss forward pass (FwP): Insert hook from left to right behind front vertical bar of stitch indicated, yo and pull up a lp.

TwTss return pass: Work as for Tss RetP.

TUNISIAN DECREASE (TSS DEC)

Tss Dec forward pass (FwP): Work as for Tss FwP.

Tss Dec return pass (RetP): Work as for Tss RetP to stitch indicated, yo and pull through 3 lps on hook.

TUNISIAN INCREASE (TSS INC)

Tss Inc forward pass (FwP): Tks and Tss in stitch indicated.

TUNISIAN STITCH PATTERN

Ch a multiple of 4 sts plus 2.

Row 1: Forward Pass (FwdP): Pull up lp in 2nd ch from hook and each across.

Row 1: Return Pass (RetP): Work lps off as normal (see Stitch Guide).

Row 2: FwdP: (lp on hook counts as first st), Tps in next st, *Tss in next st, TwTss in next st, Tps in next 2 sts; rep from * across to last 4 sts, tss in next st, TwTss in next st, Tps in next st, tss in last st.

Row 2: RetP: Work lps off as normal.

Rows 3 and 4: Rep Row 2 twice more.

Row 5: Fwd: Tss in each st across.

Row 5: RetP: Work lps off as normal.

Rep Rows 2–5 to desired length.

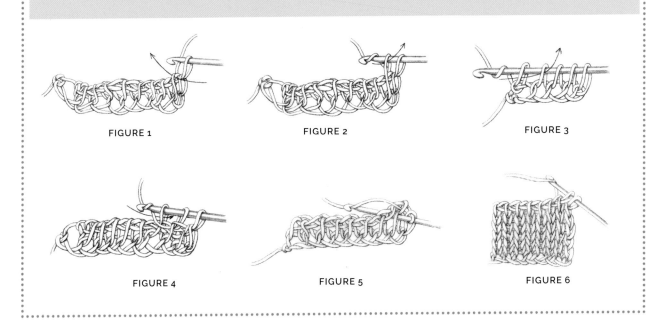

FIGURE 1

FIGURE 2

FIGURE 3

FIGURE 4

FIGURE 5

FIGURE 6

Back Panel

Ch 42 (46, 50, 54).

Beg Tunisian Stitch Pattern (see Stitch Guide or chart) and work for 16 (16, 20, 20) rows total—42 (46, 50, 54) sts.

ARMHOLE SHAPING

Size Newborn–6 Months only
Row 1: FwdP: Tps in next st and draw lp through lp on hook, Tss in each st across to last 2 sts, leave remaining sts unworked, which will be finished off later.

Sizes 6–12 (12–18) Months only
Row 1: FwdP: Tps in next st and draw lp through lp on hook, Tss in next st and draw lp through lp on hook, TwTss in next st and draw lp through lp on hook, Tss in each st across to last 4 (4) sts, leave remaining sts unworked, which will be finished off later.

Size 18–24 Months only
Row 1: FwdP: Tps in next st and draw lp through lp on hook, Tss in next st and draw lp through lp on hook, TwTss in next st and draw lp through lp on hook. [Tps in next st and draw lp through lp on hook] twice, Tss in each st across to last 6 sts, leave remaining sts unworked, which will be finished off later.

All Sizes
Row 1: RetP: Yo, draw lp through 2 lps on hook, work lps off as normal to last 2 sts, draw lp through last 3 lps on hook (dec made)—36 (36, 40, 40) sts.

Row 2: FwdP (first lp on hook counts as st throughout): Tss in next st, Tps in next 5 (3, 3, 1) sts, *Tss in next st, TwTss in next st, Tps in next 2 sts; rep from * across to last 9 (7, 7, 9) sts, Tss in next st, TwTss in next st, Tps in next 5 (3, 3, 1) sts, Tss in last 2 sts.

Row 2: RetP: Yo, draw lp through 2 lps on hook, work lps off as normal to last 2 sts, draw lp through last 3 lps on hook—34 (34, 38, 38) sts.

Row 3: FwdP: Tss in next st, Tps in next 4 (2, 2, 0) sts, *Tss in next st, TwTss in next st, Tps in next 2 sts; rep from * across to last 8 (6, 6, 4) sts, Tss in next st, TwTss in next st, Tps in next 4 (2, 2, 0) sts, Tss in last 2 sts.

Row 3: RetP: Yo, draw lp through 2 lps on hook, work lps off as normal to last 2 sts, draw lp through last 3 lps on hook—32 (32, 36, 36) sts.

Row 4: FwdP: Tps in next 4 (2, 2, 0) sts, *Tss in next st, TwTss in next st, Tps in next 2 sts; rep from * across to last 7 (5, 5, 3) sts, Tss in next st, TwTss in next st, Tps in next 4 (2, 2, 0) sts, Tss in last st.

Row 4: RetP: Work lps off as normal.

Row 5: FwdP: Tss in each st across.

Row 5: RetP: Work lps off as normal.

Sizes Newborn–6 Months (6–12 Months) only
Rows 6–12: Rep Row 4 three times, rep Row 5 once, rep Row 4 three times.

Sizes 12–18 (18–24 Months) only
Rows 6–14: [Rep Row 4 three times, rep Row 5 once] twice, rep Row 4 once.

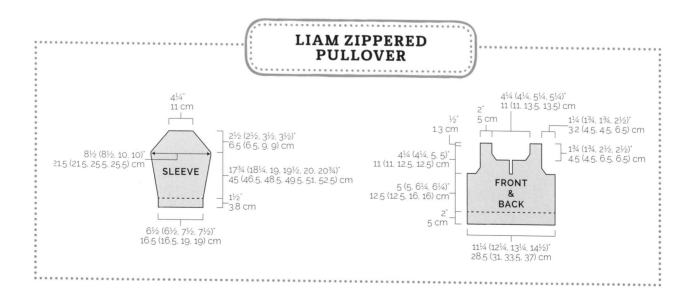

LIAM ZIPPERED PULLOVER

SLEEVE
4¼"
11 cm

2½ (2½, 3½, 3½)"
6.5 (6.5, 9, 9) cm

8½ (8½, 10, 10)"
21.5 (21.5, 25.5, 25.5) cm

17¾ (18¼, 19, 19½, 20, 20¾)"
45 (46.5, 48.5, 49.5, 51, 52.5) cm

1½"
3.8 cm

6½ (6½, 7½, 7½)"
16.5 (16.5, 19, 19) cm

FRONT & BACK
4¼ (4¼, 5¼, 5¼)"
11 (11, 13.5, 13.5) cm

2"
5 cm

½"
1.3 cm

1¼ (1¾, 1¾, 2½)"
3.2 (4.5, 4.5, 6.5) cm

1¾ (1¾, 2½, 2½)"
4.5 (4.5, 6.5, 6.5) cm

4¼ (4¼, 5, 5)"
11 (11, 12.5, 12.5) cm

5 (5, 6¼, 6¼)"
12.5 (12.5, 16, 16) cm

2"
5 cm

11¼ (12¼, 13¼, 14½)"
28.5 (31, 33.5, 37) cm

Sizes 6–12 (12-18) Months only

Row 13 (15): FwdP: Tps in next 2 sts, Tss in next st, TwTss in next st, Tps in next 2 sts, Tss in last st, leave remaining sts unworked.

Row 13 (15): RetP: Work lps off as normal—8 (8) sts.

Row 14 (16): FwdP: Tps in next 2 sts, Tss in next st, TwTss in next st, Tps in next 2 sts, Tss in last st.

Row 14 (16): RetP: Work lps off as normal.

Last row: Sl st in each st across. Fasten off.

Size 18–24 Months only

Row 15: FwdP: Tss in next st, TwTss in next st, Tps in next 2 sts, Tss in next st, TwTss in next st, Tss in last st, leave remaining sts unworked.

Row 15: RetP: Work lps off as normal—8 sts.

Row 16: FwdP: Tss in next st, TwTss in next st, Tps in next 2 sts, Tss in next st, TwTss in next st, Tss in last st.

Row 16: RetP: Work lps off as normal—8 sts.

Last row: Sl st in each st across. Fasten off.

ARMHOLE SHAPING (LEFT) FINISHING

Note: This is the bind-off finishing for the sts unworked at the end of Row 1 of armhole shaping.

Join yarn with sl st to last st on Row 1 of armhole shaping:

RIGHT SHOULDER

Newborn–6 Months only

Row 13: FwdP: Tps in next 4 sts, Tss in next st, TwTss in next st, Tss in last st, leave remaining sts unworked.

Row 13: RetP: Work lps off as normal –8 sts.

Row 14: FwdP: Tps in next 4 sts, Tss in next st, TwTss in next st, Tss in last st.

Row 14: RetP: Work lps off as normal.

Last row: Sl st in each st across. Fasten off.

TUNISIAN STITCH PATTERN

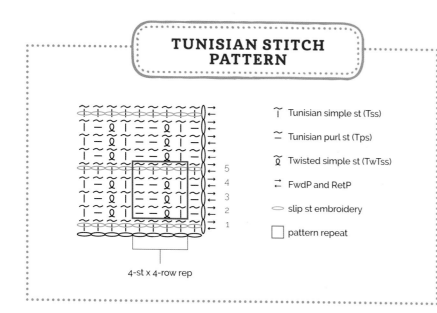

⊤	Tunisian simple st (Tss)
∼	Tunisian purl st (Tps)
℺	Twisted simple st (TwTss)
⇄	FwdP and RetP
⬭	slip st embroidery
☐	pattern repeat

4-st x 4-row rep

Size Newborn-6 Months only

Row 1: FwdP: Tps in next st and draw lp through lp on hook, Tss in last st and draw lp through lp on hook. Fasten off. Reinsert hook into working loop to continue back.

Sizes 6-12 (12-18) Months only

Row 1: FwdP: Tss in next st and draw lp through lp on hook, TwTss in next st and draw lp through lp on hook, Tps in next st and draw lp through lp on hook, Tss in last st and draw lp through lp on hook. Fasten off. Reinsert hook into working loop to continue back.

Size 18-24 Months only

Row 1: FwdP: [Tps in next st and draw through lp on hook] twice, Tss in next st and draw lp through lp on hook, TwTss in next st and draw lp through lp on hook, Tps in next st and draw lp through lp on hook, Tss in last st and draw lp through lp on hook. Fasten off. Reinsert hook into working loop to continue back.

BACK NECK

Sizes Newborn-6 Months (18-24 Months) only

Join yarn with sl st to end of Row 13 (15) of right shoulder, Tps in next st and draw through lp on hook, *Tss in next st and draw through lp on hook, TwTss in next st and draw through lp on hook, [Tps in next st and draw through lp on hook] twice; rep from * across to last 11 sts, Tss in next st and draw through lp on hook, TwTss in next st and draw through lp on hook, Tps in next st and draw through lp on hook. Work left shoulder on rem 8 sts.

Sizes 6-12 (12-18) Months only

Join yarn with sl st to end of Row 13 (15) of right shoulder, * TwTss in next st and draw through lp on hook, [Tps in next st and draw through lp on hook] twice, Tss in next st and draw through lp on hook; rep from * across to last 8 sts. Work left shoulder on rem 8 sts.

LEFT SHOULDER

Size Newborn-6 Months only

Row 13: FwdP: Tss in next st, TwTss in next st, Tps in next 4 sts, Tss in last st.

Row 13: RetP: Work lps off as normal—8 sts.

Row 14: FwdP: Tss in next st, TwTss in next st, Tps in next 4 sts, Tss in last st.

Row 14: RetP: Work lps off as normal.

Last row: Sl st in each st across. Fasten off.

Size 6-12 Months only

Row 13: FwdP: Tss in next st, Tps in next 2 sts, Tss in next st, TwTss in next st, Tps in next 2 sts, Tss in last st.

Row 13: RetP: Work lps off as normal—8 sts.

Row 14 (16): FwdP: Tps in next 2 sts, Tss in next st, TwTss in next st, Tps in next 2 sts, Tss in last st.

Row 14 (16): RetP: Work lps off as normal.

Last row: Sl st in each st across. Fasten off.

Size 12-18 Months only

Row 15: FwdP: [TwTss in next st, Tps in next 2 sts, Tss in next st] twice.

Row 15: RetP: Work lps off as normal—8 sts.

Row 16: FwdP: Tps in next 2 sts, Tss in next st, TwTss in next st, Tps in next 2 sts, Tss in last sts.

Row 16: RetP: Work lps off as normal.

Last row: Sl st in each st across. Fasten off.

Size 18-24 Months only

Row 15: FwdP: Tps in next st, Tss in next st, TwTss in next st, Tps in next

2 sts, Tss in next st, TwTss in next st, Tss in last st.

Row 15: RetP: Work lps off as normal—8 sts.

Row 16: FwdP: Tss in next st, TwTss in next st, Tps in next 2 sts, Tss in next st, TwTss in next st, Tss in last st.

Row 16: RetP: Work lps off as normal.

Last row: Sl st in each st across. Fasten off.

Front Panel

Rep instructions for back panel to armhole shaping—42 (46, 50, 54) sts.

ARMHOLE AND LEFT FRONT NECK SHAPING

Size Newborn–6 Months only

Row 1: FwdP: Tps in next st and draw lp through lp on hook, Tss in next 18 sts, leave remaining sts unworked.

Row 1: RetP: Work lps off as normal to last 2 sts, draw lp through last 3 lps on hook *(dec made)*—17 sts.

Row 2: FwdP (first lp on hook counts as st throughout): Tss in next st, Tps in next 6 sts, *Tss in next st, TwTss in next st, Tps in next 2 sts; rep from * across to last 2 sts, Tss in last 2 sts.

Row 2: RetP: Work lps off as normal to last 2 sts, draw lp through last 3 lps on hook—16 sts.

Row 3: FwdP: Tss in next st, Tps in next 4 sts, *Tss in next st, TwTss in next st, Tps in next 2 sts; rep from * across to last 2 sts, Tss in last 2 sts.

Row 3: RetP: Work lps off as normal to last 2 sts, draw lp through last 3 lps on hook—15 sts.

Row 4: FwdP: Tps in next 4 sts, *Tss in next st, TwTss in next st, Tps in next 2 sts; rep from * across to last 2 sts, Tss in last 2 sts.

Row 4: RetP: Work lps off as normal.

Row 5: FwdP: Tss in each st across.

Row 5: RetP: Work lps off as normal.

Rows 6–8: Rep Row 4 three times.

Row 9: FwdP: Tss in next 10 sts across.

Row 9: RetP: Yo, draw lp through 2 lps on hook, work lps off as normal—10 sts.

Row 10: FwdP: Tps in next 4 sts, Tss in next st, TwTss in next st, Tps in next st, Tss in next 2 sts.

Row 10: RetP: Yo, draw lp through 2 lps on hook, work lps off as normal—9 sts.

Row 11: FwdP: Tps in next 4 sts, Tss in next st, TwTss in next st, Tss in next 2 sts.

Row 11: RetP: Yo, draw lp through 2 lps on hook, work lps off as normal—8 sts.

Row 12: FwdP: Tps in next 4 sts, Tss in next st, TwTss in next st, Tss in last st.

Sizes 6–12 (12–18) Months only

Row 1: FwdP: Tps in next st and draw lp through lp on hook, Tss in next st and draw lp through lp on hook, TwTss in next st and draw lp through lp on hook, Tss in next 18 (20) sts, leave remaining sts unworked.

Row 1: RetP: Work lps off as normal to last 2 sts, draw lp through last 3 lps on hook (dec made)—17 (19) sts.

Row 2: FwdP (first lp on hook counts as st throughout): *Tss in next st, TwTss in next st, Tps in next 2 sts; rep from * across to last 2 sts, Tss in last 2 sts.

Row 2: RetP: Work lps off as normal to last 2 sts, draw lp through last 3 lps on hook—16 (18) sts.

Row 3: FwdP: TwTss in next st, Tps in next 2 sts, * Tss in next st, TwTss in next st, Tps in next 2 sts; rep from * across to last 2 sts, Tss in last 2 sts.

Row 3: RetP: Work lps off as normal to last 2 sts, draw lp through last 3 lps on hook—15 (17) sts.

Row 4: FwdP: Tps in next 2 sts, *Tss in next st, TwTss in next st, Tps in next 2 sts; rep from * across to last 2 sts, Tss in last 2 sts.

Row 4: RetP: Work lps off as normal.

Row 5: FwdP: Tss in each st across.

Row 5: RetP: Work lps off as normal.

Rows 6-8: Rep Row 4 three times.

Row 9: FwdP: Tss in next 10 sts across.

Row 9: RetP: Yo, draw lp through 2 lps on hook, work lps off as normal—10 sts.

Row 10: FwdP: Tps in next 2 sts, Tss in next st, TwTss in next st, Tps in next st, Tss in next 2 sts.

Row 10: RetP: Yo, draw lp through 2 lps on hook, work lps off as normal—9 sts.

Row 11: FwdP: Tps in next 2 sts, Tss in next st, TwTss in next st, Tps in next 2 sts, Tss in next 2 sts.

Row 11: RetP: Yo, draw lp through 2 lps on hook, work lps off as normal—8 sts.

Row 12: FwdP: Tps in next 2 sts, Tss in next st, TwTss in next st, Tps in next 2 sts, Tss in last st.

Size 18-24 Months only

Row 1: FwdP: Tps in next st and draw lp through lp on hook, Tss in next st and draw lp through lp on hook, TwTss in next st and draw lp through lp on hook, [Tps in next st and draw up a lp] twice, Tss in next 20 sts, leave remaining sts unworked.

Row 1: RetP: Work lps off as normal to last 2 sts, draw lp through last 3 lps on hook (dec made)—19 sts.

Row 2: FwdP (first lp on hook counts as st throughout): Tps in next 2 sts, *Tss in next st, TwTss in next st, Tps in next 2 sts; rep from * across to last 2 sts, Tss in last 2 sts.

Row 2: RetP: Work lps off as normal to last 2 sts, draw lp through last 3 lps on hook—18 sts.

Row 3: FwdP: Tps in next st, *Tss in next st, TwTss in next st, Tps in next 2 sts; rep from * across to last 2 sts, Tss in last 2 sts.

Row 3: RetP: Work lps off as normal to last 2 sts, draw lp through last 3 lps on hook—17 sts.

Row 4: FwdP: *Tss in next st, TwTss in next st, Tps in next 2 sts; rep from * across to last 2 sts, Tss in last 2 sts.

Row 4: RetP: Work lps off as normal.

Row 5: FwdP: Tss in each st across.

Row 5: RetP: Work lps off as normal.

Rows 6-8: Rep Row 4 three times.

Row 9: FwdP: Tss in next 10 sts across.

Row 9: RetP: Yo, draw lp through 2 lps on hook, work lps off as normal—10 sts.

Row 10: FwdP: Tss in next st, TwTss in next st, Tps in next 2 sts, Tss in next st, TwTss in next st, Tss in last st.

Row 10: RetP: Yo, draw lp through 2 lps on hook, work lps off as normal—9 sts.

Row 11: FwdP: Tss in next st, TwTss in next st, Tps in next 2 sts, Tss in next st, TwTss in next st, Tss in last st.

Row 11: RetP: Yo, draw lp through 2 lps on hook, work lps off as normal—8 sts.

Row 12: FwdP: Tss in next st, TwTss in next st, Tps in next 2 sts, Tss in next st, TwTss in next st, Tss in last st.

All Sizes
Row 12: RetP: Work lps off as normal.

Rows 13 and 14 (13 and 14, 13-16, 13-16): Rep Row 12.

Last row: Sl st in each st across. Fasten off.

ARMHOLE AND RIGHT FRONT NECK SHAPING
All Sizes

Row 1: FwdP: Join yarn with sl st to end of Row 1 of left armhole shaping, [Tps in next st and draw through lp on hook] twice—2 sts BO. Tps in each st across to last 2 sts—18 (18, 20, 20) sts. Leave rem sts unworked, which will be finished off later.

Row 1: RetP: Yo, draw lp through 2 lps on hook, work lps off as normal (*dec made*)—17 (17, 19, 19) sts.

Size Newborn–6 Months only

Row 2: FwdP (first lp on hook counts as st throughout): TwTss in next st, Tps in next 2 sts, *Tss in next st, TwTss in next st, Tps in next 2 sts; rep from * across to last 5 sts, Tps in next 3 sts, Tss in last 2 sts.

Row 2: RetP: Yo, draw lp through 2 lps on hook, work lps off as normal to last st, Tss in last st—16 sts.

Row 3: FwdP: TwTss in next st, Tps in next 2 sts, *Tss in next st, TwTss in next st, Tps in next 2 sts; rep from * across to last 4 sts, Tps in next 2 sts, Tss in last 2 sts.

Row 3: RetP: Yo, draw lp through 2 lps on hook, work lps off as normal to last st, Tss in last st—15 sts.

Row 4: FwdP: TwTss in next st, Tps in next 2 sts *Tss in next st, TwTss in next st, Tps in next 2 sts; rep from * across to last 3 sts, Tps in next 2 ats, Tss in last st.

Row 4: RetP: Work lps off as normal.

Row 5: FwdP: Tss in each st across.

Row 5: RetP: Work lps off as normal.

Rows 6–8: Rep Row 4 three times.

Row 9: FwdP: TwTss in next st and draw lp through lp on hook, [Tps in next st and draw lp through lp on hook] twice, Tss in each st across—11 sts.

Row 9: RetP: Work lps off as normal to last 2 sts, draw lp through last 3 lps on hook—10 sts.

Row 10: FwdP: Tps in next st, Tss in next st, TwTss in next st, Tps in next 4 sts, Tss in last st.

Row 10: RetP: Work lps off as normal to last 2 sts, draw lp through last 3 lps on hook—9 sts.

Row 11: FwdP: Tps in next st, Tss in next st, TwTss in next st, Tps in next 4 sts, Tss in last st.

Row 11: RetP: Work lps off as normal to last 2 sts, draw lp through last 3 lps on hook—8 sts.

Row 12: FwdP: Tss in next st, TwTss in next st, Tps in next 4 sts, Tss in last st.

Row 9: RetP: Work lps off as normal to last 2 sts, draw lp through last 3 lps on hook—10 sts.

Row 10: FwdP: [Tss in next st, TwTss in next st, Tps in next 2 sts] twice, Tss in last st.

Row 10: RetP: Work lps off as normal to last 2 sts, draw lp through last 3 lps on hook—9 sts.

Row 11: FwdP: TwTss in next st, Tps in next 2 sts, Tss in next st, TwTss in next st, Tps in next 2 sts, Tss in last st.

Row 11: RetP: Work lps off as normal to last 2 sts, draw lp through last 3 lps on hook—8 sts.

Row 12: FwdP: Tps in next 2 sts, Tss in next st, TwTss in next st, Tps in next 2 sts, Tss in last st.

Size 12–18 Months only

Row 2: FwdP (first lp on hook counts as st throughout): TwTss in next st, Tps in next 2 sts, *Tss in next st, TwTss in next st, Tps in next 2 sts; rep from * across to last 3 sts, Tss in last 3 sts.

Row 2: RetP: Yo, draw lp through 2 lps on hook, work lps off as normal to last st, Tss in last st—18 sts.

Row 3: FwdP: TwTss in next st, Tps in next 2 sts, *Tss in next st, TwTss in next st, Tps in next 2 sts; rep from * across to last 2 sts, Tss in last 2 sts.

Row 3: RetP: Yo, draw lp through 2 lps on hook, work lps off as normal to last st, Tss in last st—17 sts.

Row 4: FwdP: TwTss in next st, Tps in next 2 sts, *Tss in next st, TwTss in next st, Tps in next 2 sts; rep from * across to last st, Tss in last st.

Size 6–12 Months only

Row 2: FwdP (first lp on hook counts as st throughout): Tps in next st, *Tss in next st, TwTss in next st, Tps in next 2 sts; rep from * across to last 3 sts, Tss in last 3 sts.

Row 2: RetP: Yo, draw lp through 2 lps on hook, work lps off as normal to last st, Tss in last st—16 sts.

Row 3: FwdP: Tps in next st, *Tss in next st, TwTss in next st, Tps in next 2 sts; rep from * across to last 2 sts, Tss in last 2 sts.

Row 3: RetP: Yo, draw lp through 2 lps on hook, work lps off as normal to last st, Tss in last st—15 sts.

Row 4: FwdP: Tps in next st, *Tss in next st, TwTss in next st, Tps in next 2 sts; rep from * across to last st, Tss in last st.

Row 4: RetP: Work lps off as normal.

Row 5: FwdP: Tss in each st across.

Row 5: RetP: Work lps off as normal.

Rows 6–8: Rep Row 4 three times.

Row 9: FwdP: Tps in next st and draw lp through lp on hook, Tss in next st and draw lp through lp on hook, TwTss in next st and draw lp through lp on hook, Tss in each st across—11 sts.

Row 4: RetP: Work lps off as normal.

Row 5: FwdP: Tss in each st across.

Row 5: RetP: Work lps off as normal.

Rows 6–8: Rep Row 4 three times.

Row 9: FwdP: TwTss in next st and draw lp through lp on hook, [Tps in next st and draw lp through lp on hook] twice, Tss in next st and draw lp through lp on hook, TwTss in next st and draw lp through lp on hook, Tss in each st across—11 sts.

Row 9: RetP: Work lps off as normal to last 2 sts, draw lp through last 3 lps on hook—10 sts.

Row 10: FwdP: [Tss in next st, TwTss in next st, Tps in next 2 sts] twice, Tss in last st.

Row 10: RetP: Work lps off as normal to last 2 sts, draw lp through last 3 lps on hook—9 sts.

Row 11: FwdP: TwTss in next st, Tps in next 2 sts, Tss in next st, TwTss in next st, Tps in next 2 sts, Tss in last st.

Row 11: RetP: Work lps off as normal to last 2 sts, draw lp through last 3 lps on hook—8 sts.

Row 12: FwdP: Tps in next 2 sts, Tss in next st, TwTss in next st, Tps in next 2 sts, Tss in last st.

Size 18–24 Months only
Row 2: FwdP (first lp on hook counts as st throughout): Tps in next st, *Tss in next st, TwTss in next st, Tps in next 2 sts; rep from * across, ending last rep with Tss in last st.

Row 2: RetP: Yo, draw lp through 2 lps on hook, work lps off as normal to last st, Tss in last st—18 sts.

Row 3: FwdP: Tps in next st, *Tss in next st, TwTss in next st, Tps in next 2 sts; rep from * across to last 4 sts, Tss in next st, TwTss in next st, Tps in last 2 sts.

Row 3: RetP: Yo, draw lp through 2 lps on hook, work lps off as normal to last st, Tss in last st—17 sts.

Row 4: FwdP: Tps in next st, *Tss in next st, TwTss in next st, Tps in next 2 sts; rep from * across to last 3 sts, Tss in next st, TwTss in next st, Tss in last st.

Row 4: RetP: Work lps off as normal.

Row 5: FwdP: Tss in each st across.

Row 5: RetP: Work lps off as normal.

Rows 6–8: Rep Row 4 three times.

Row 9: FwdP: Tps in next st and draw lp through lp on hook, *Tss in next st and draw lp through lp on hook, TwTss in next st and draw lp through lp on hook, [Tps in next st and draw lp through lp on hook] twice, Tss in each st across—11 sts.

Row 9: RetP: Work lps off as normal to last 2 sts, draw lp through last 3 lps on hook—10 sts.

Row 10: FwdP: Tps in next 2 sts, Tss in next st, TwTss in next st, Tps in next 2 sts, Tss in next st, TwTss in next st, Tss in last st.

Row 10: RetP: Work lps off as normal to last 2 sts, draw lp through last 3 lps on hook—9 sts.

Row 11: FwdP: Tps in next st, Tss in next st, TwTss in next st, Tps in next 2 sts, Tss in next st, TwTss in next st, Tss in last st.

Row 11: RetP: Work lps off as normal to last 2 sts, draw lp through last 3 lps on hook—8 sts.

Row 12: FwdP: Tss in next st, TwTss in next st, Tps in next 2 sts, Tss in next st, TwTss in next st, Tss in last st.

All Sizes
Row 12: RetP: Work lps off as normal.

Rows 13 and 14 (13 and 14, 13–16, 13–16): Rep Row 12.

Last row: Sl st in each st across. Fasten off.

ARMHOLE SHAPING (RIGHT) FINISHING
Note: This is the bind-off finishing for the sts unworked at the end of Row 1 of armhole shaping.

Join yarn with sl st to last st on Row 1 of armhole shaping and work as for back left armhole finishing.

Sleeves
Ch 24 (24, 28, 28).

Row 1: FwdP: Pull up lp in 2nd ch from hook and in each ch across.

Row 1: RetP: Work lps off as normal—24 (24, 28, 28) sts.

Rows 2–4: FwdP: (Lp on hook counts as first st), *Tps in next 2 sts, Tss in next st, TwTss in next st; rep from * across to last 3 sts, Tps in next 2 sts, Tss in last st.

Rows 2–4: RetP: Work lps off as normal.

Row 5: (inc) FwdP: Tss in first st (inc made), Tss in each st across to last st, (Tks, Tss) in last st (*inc made*).

Row 5: RetP: Work lps off as normal—26 (26, 30, 30) sts.

Rows 6–8: FwdP: * TwTss in next st, Tps in next 2 sts, Tss in next st; rep from * across to last st, Tss in last st.

Rows 6–8: RetP: Work lps off as normal.

Row 9: (inc) Rep Row 5—28 (28, 32, 32) sts.

Rows 10–12: FwdP: *Tss in next st, TwTss in next st, Tps in next 2 sts: rep from * across to last 3 sts, Tss in next st, TwTss in next st, Tss in last st.

Rows 10–12: RetP: Work lps off as normal.

Row 13: (inc) Rep Row 5—30 (30, 34, 34) sts.

Rows 14–16: FwdP: Tps in next st, *Tss in next st, TwTss in next st, Tps in next 2 sts; rep from * across to last 4 sts, Tss in next st, TwTss in next st, Tps in next st, Tss in last st.

Rows 14–16: RetP: Work lps off as normal.

Row 17: (inc) Rep Row 5—32 (32, 36, 36) sts.

Rows 18 and 19 (18 and 19, 18–20, 18–20): Rep Row 2 two (three) times.

Sizes 12–18 (18–24) Months only
Row 21: (inc) Rep Row 5—38 (38) sts.

Rows 22 and 23: Rep Row 6 twice.

CAP SHAPING
Sizes Newborn–6 Months (6–12 Months) only
Row 1: FwdP: *Tps in next 2 sts, Tss in next st, TwTss in next st; rep from * to last 3 sts, Tps in next 2 sts, Tss in last st.

Row 1: RetP: Yo, draw lp through 2 lps on hook, work lps off as normal to last 2 sts, draw lp through last 3 lps on hook—30 sts.

Row 2: FwdP: Tss in each st across.

Row 2: RetP: Yo, draw lp through 2 lps on hook, work lps off as normal to last 2 sts, draw lp through last 3 lps on hook—28 sts.

Row 3: FwdP: *Tss in next st, TwTss in next st, Tps in next 2 sts; rep from * to

last 3 sts, Tss in next st, TwTss in next st, Tss in last st.

Row 3: RetP: Yo, draw lp through 2 lps on hook, work lps off as normal to last 2 sts, draw lp through last 3 lps on hook—26 sts.

Row 4: FwdP: *TwTss in next st, Tps in next 2 sts, Tss in next st; rep from * to last st, Tss in last st.

Row 4: RetP: Yo, draw lp through 2 lps on hook, work lps off as normal to last 2 sts, draw lp through last 3 lps on hook—24 sts.

Rows 5–8: Rep Rows 1–4 once more—16 sts.

Last row: *[Tps in next st and draw through lp on hook] twice, Tss in next st and draw through lp on hook, TwTss in next st and draw through lp on hook; rep from * to last 3 sts, [Tps in next st and draw through lp on hook] twice, Tss in last st and draw through lp on hook. Fasten off.

Sizes 12–18 (18–24) Months only

Row 1: FwdP: Tss in next st, *Tps in next 2 sts, Tss in next st, TwTss in next st; rep from * to last 4 sts, Tps in next 2 sts, Tss in last 2 sts.

Row 1: RetP: Yo, draw lp through 2 lps on hook, work lps off as normal to last 2 sts, draw lp through last 3 lps on hook—36 sts.

Row 2: FwdP: Tss in each st across.

Row 2: RetP: Yo, draw lp through 2 lps on hook, work lps off as normal to last 2 sts, draw lp through last 3 lps on hook—34 sts.

Row 3: FwdP: Tss in next st, *Tss in next st, TwTss in next st, Tps in next 2 sts; rep from * to last 4 sts, Tss in next st, TwTss in next st, Tss in last 2 sts.

Row 3: RetP: Yo, draw lp through 2 lps on hook, work lps off as normal to last 2 sts, draw lp through last 3 lps on hook—32 sts.

Row 4: FwdP: Tss in next st, *TwTss in next st, Tps in next 2 sts, Tss in next st; rep from * to last 2 sts, Tss in last 2 sts.

Row 4: RetP: Yo, draw lp through 2 lps on hook, work lps off as normal to last 2 sts, draw lp through last 3 lps on hook—30 sts.

Rows 5–11: Rep Rows 1–4 once, rep Rows 1–3 once more—16 sts.

Last row: *Tss in next st and draw through lp on hook, TwTss in next st and draw through lp on hook, [Tps in next st and draw through lp on hook] twice; rep from * to last 3 sts, Tss in next st and draw through lp on hook, TwTss in next st and draw through lp on hook, Tss in last st and draw through lp on hook. Fasten off.

Finishing

Pin front and back panels and sleeves to schematic size, spray with water, and allow to dry.

Sl st embroider (see Glossary) on horizontal lines (patt Row 5) by joining yarn to side edge at any Tss stitch. Sl st chain across panel by inserting hook from RS to WS and pulling up a lp from the back to sl st over each Tss, being careful not to pucker fabric. Rep across panel. Fasten off. Weave in ends.

Place RS of back and front panels tog. Using running stitch (see Glossary), sew the side seams and turn RS out. Set in sleeve with RS facing. Seam in sleeve with running stitch. Rep on underarm seam.

BOTTOM RIBBING

Join yarn to bottom edge of back with sl st and ch 9.

Row 1: Sc in 2nd ch from hook, sc in each ch across, sl st twice to bottom edge (once to join and once to act as turning ch), turn—8 sts.

Row 2: Sk both sl sts, sc blo in each sc across, turn.

Row 3: Ch 1, sc blo in each sc across, sl st twice to edge, turn.

Rep Rows 2 and 3 around edge to beg. Fasten off. Whipstitch (see Glossary) first and last rows tog.

CUFFS

Join yarn to cuff edge at seam and ch 7. Rep instructions as for bottom ribbing over 6 sts.

COLLAR

Join yarn to neck edge at opening, ch 11. Rep instructions as for bottom ribbing over 10 sts to opposite side, do not fasten off. Sc evenly down and around neck zipper opening. Fasten off. Weave in ends.

Pin zipper to neck opening. Backstitch (see Glossary) zipper in place with matching thread.

Oskar
CAR SEAT SWADDLE

DESIGNED BY TERRI L. KELLER

A heavy coat can be too warm and bulky to wear while riding in a car seat. This project is designed to allow the car seat straps to buckle and the arms to be swaddled without adding bulk between the baby and the harness straps. After the car ride, baby can stay swaddled and warm in this cozy, smooshy, and fun-to-crochet wrap.

FINISHED SIZE

Instructions are written for size 3–9 months. Pattern can easily be lengthened for larger sizes by adding extra rnds and rows.

Main body circumference: 30" (76 cm).

Main body length: 12" (30.5 cm).

Arm wrap wingspan: 38" (96.5 cm).

Arm wrap length: 8½" (21.5 cm).

Hood length: 7" (18 cm).

YARN

Sportweight (#2 Fine).

Shown here: Malabrigo Arroyo (100% superwash merino; 335 yd [306 m]/3½ oz [100 g]): #131 sand bank, 3 skeins.

HOOKS

Size G/6 (4 mm) (for main body and hood).

Size K/10½ (6.5 mm) (for swaddle wrap).

Adjust hook size if necessary to obtain correct gauge.

NOTIONS

Two 1" (25 mm) buttons; ⅝–¾" (1.5–2 cm) wide × 36" (91.5 cm) long ribbon for drawstring; locking st markers or knitting marking pins; yarn needle.

GAUGE

16 hdc and 14 rows = 4" (10 cm) in main body pattern using size G/6 (4 mm) hook.

5½ star groups and 8 rws = 4" (10 cm) in Star Stitch pattern using size K/10½ (6.5 mm) hook.

NOTES

Swaddle is worked in three sections: Main body is worked in the rnd, arm wrap is worked flat then slip stitched to main body, then hood is worked flat and seamed.

STAR STITCH PATTERN

Foundation row: Ch 1, *ch 1 drawing up ¼" (6 mm) lp, yo and insert hook in ch (just made), yo and draw up ¼" (6 mm) lp, hold strand of working yarn to stay the same length as the lps on hook, yo and draw through all 3 lps on hook, insert hook under strand of yarn held, yo and draw through strand and lp on hook (sl st made), ch 1—*one foundation group made*; rep from * for number of groups indicated, turn to work along groups.

Row 1: (turning group worked at beg of row) Draw up ¼" (6 mm) lp on hook, yo and draw up ¼" (6 mm) length lp bet first and 2nd groups, hold strand of working yarn to stay the same length as the lps on hook, yo and draw through all 3 lps on hook, yo and draw through under strand of yarn held, and lp on hook (sl st made), ch 1—*turning (beg) group made*.

Row 1: (Star Stitch pattern worked after beg turning group) *Draw up a ¼" (6 mm) lp, yo and insert hook in same st of group just completed, yo and draw up ¼" (6 mm) lp, yo and insert hook in next ch st (bet next 2 groups), yo and draw up ¼" (6 mm) lp, hold strand of working yarn to the same ¼" (6 mm) length, yo and draw through all 5 lps on hook, insert hook under strand of yarn held, yo and sl st through both lps on hook, ch 1—*one star made*; rep from * across over fnd groups, ending in beg first ch of fnd row, turn.

Row 2: (turning group worked at beg of row) Draw up ¼" (6 mm) lp on hook, yo and draw up ¼" (6 mm) length lp same st of group last completed (point of star), hold strand of working yarn to stay the same length as the lps on hook, yo and draw through all 3 lps on hook, yo and draw through under strand of yarn held, and lp on hook (sl st made), ch 1—*turning (beg) group made*.

Row 2: (Star Stitch pattern worked after beg turning group) *Draw up a ¼" (6 mm) lp, yo and insert hook in same st of group just completed, yo and draw up ¼" (6 mm) lp, yo and insert hook in next ch st (at point of star), yo and draw up ¼" (6 mm) lp, hold strand of working yarn to the same ¼" (6 mm) length, yo and draw through all 5 lps on hook, insert hook under strand of yarn held, yo and sl st through both lps on hook, ch 1—*one star made*; rep from * across, ending in beg first ch of prev row, turn.

Rep Row 2 for pattern.

Main Body (Front and Back)

With size G/6 (4 mm) hook, ch 120, sl st in beg ch to join in the rnd, being careful not to twist work.

Rnd 1: Ch 1 (does not count as st throughout), sc in each ch, sl st in beg ch to join—120 sts.

Rnd 2: (eyelet) Ch 1, *sc in next 2 sc, ch 2, sk next 2 sc; rep from * around, sl st in beg ch-1 to join—30 ch-2 sp.

Rnd 3: Ch 1, *sc in next 2 sc, 2 sc in ch-2 sp; rep from * around, sl st in beg ch-1 to join.

Rnd 4: Ch 2 (counts as first hdc), *hdc in next sc; rep from * around, sl st in top of beg ch-2 to join—120 hdc.

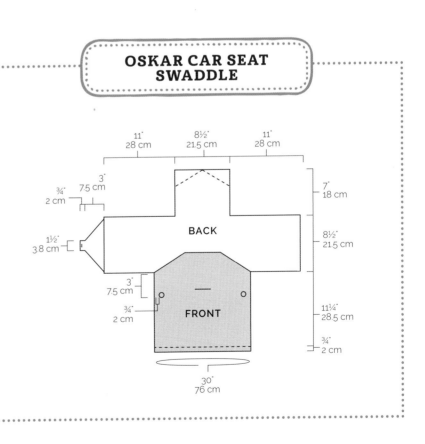

OSKAR CAR SEAT SWADDLE

Rnd 5: Ch 1, *sl st in first hdc, dc in next hdc; rep from * around, sl st in beg sl st to join.

Rep Rnds 4 and 5 for patt until piece measures 12" (30.5 cm) or desired length.

Next rnd: (buckle opening) Work 25 sts in est patt, ch 10, sk next 10 sts, work next 50 sts in patt, ch 10, sk next 10 sts, work final 25 sts in patt, sl st to beg ch to join.

Next rnd: Work even in patt across to include the ch-10 sts, sl st in beg ch to join.

Continue to work even in patt for an additional 3" (7.5 cm) or desired length, ending with Rnd 5.

FRONT FLAP
Work back and forth in rows, dec on every RS row as follows:

Row 1: (RS) Ch 2 (counts as hdc), hdc in next 39 sts, turn—40 hdc.

Row 2: Ch 1, [sl st in next hdc, dc in next hdc] across, turn.

Row 3: Ch 2 (counts as hdc), hdc2tog (see Glossary) over next 2 sts, hdc in each st to last 3 sts, hdc2tog, hdc in last st—38 hdc.

Rep Rows 2 and 3 until 22 sts remain. Fasten off.

Arm Wrap

Note: Foundation begins with ch 1 to form foundation groups.

With K/10½ (6.5 mm) hook, ch 1.

Fnd row: *Ch 1, drawing up ¼" (6 mm) lp, yo and insert hook in ch (just

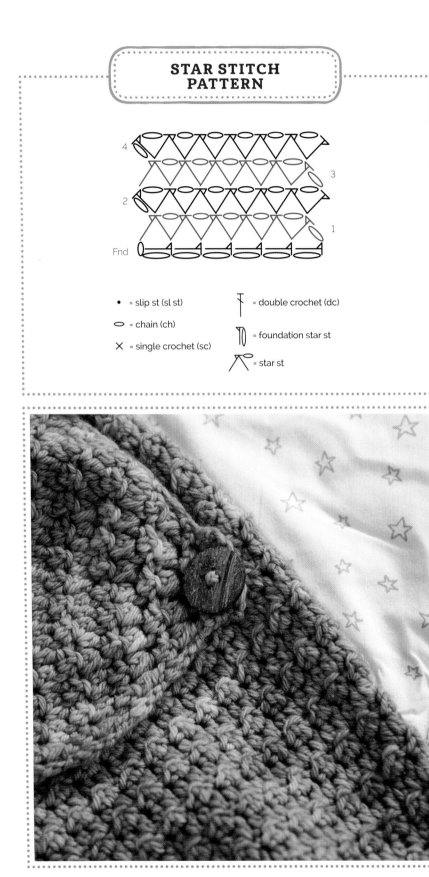

STAR STITCH PATTERN

4

3

2

1

Fnd

• = slip st (sl st)

◯ = chain (ch)

✕ = single crochet (sc)

▐ = double crochet (dc)

▐▐ = foundation star st

⋀ = star st

made), yo and draw up ¼" (6 mm) lp, hold strand of working yarn to stay the same length as the lps on hook, yo and draw through all 3 lps on hook, insert hook under strand of yarn held, yo and draw through strand and lp on hook (sl st made), ch 1—*one fnd group made*; rep from * 41 more times—42 fnd groups, turn to work along groups.

Row 1: Draw up ¼" (6 mm) lp on hook, yo and draw up ¼" (6 mm) length lp bet first and 2nd groups, hold strand of working yarn to stay the same length as the lps on hook, yo and draw through all 3 lps on hook, yo and draw through under strand of yarn held, and lp on hook (sl st made), ch 1—*turning (beg) group made.* *Draw up a ¼" (6 mm) lp, yo and insert hook in same st of group just completed, yo and draw up ¼" (6 mm) lp, yo and insert hook in next ch st (bet next 2 groups), yo and draw up ¼" (6 mm) lp, hold strand of working yarn to the same ¼" (6 mm) length, yo and draw through all 5 lps on hook, insert hook under strand of yarn held, yo and sl st through both lps on hook, ch 1—*one star made*; rep from * across over fnd groups, ending in beg first ch of fnd row, turn.

Row 2: Draw up ¼" (6 mm) lp on hook, yo and draw up ¼" (6 mm) length lp same st of group last completed (point of star), hold strand of working yarn to stay the same length as the lps on hook, yo and draw through all 3 lps on hook, yo and draw through under strand of yarn held, and lp on hook (sl st made), ch 1—*turning (beg) group made.* *Draw up a ¼" (6 mm) lp, yo and insert hook in same st of group just completed, yo and draw up ¼" (6 mm) lp, yo and insert hook in next ch st (at point of star), yo and draw up ¼" (6 mm) lp, hold strand of working

yarn to the same ¼" (6 mm) length, yo and draw through all 5 lps on hook, insert hook under strand of yarn hold, yo and sl st through both lps on hook, ch 1– *one star made*; rep from * across, ending in beg first ch of prev row, turn.

Rows 3–16: Rep Row 2. Do not fasten off. Turn to work along side edge.

SIDE EDGING

Row 1: (RS) Sc in each eyelet and leg across, turn—32 sts.

Row 2: Ch 1, *dc in next sc, sl st in next sc; rep from * across, turn.

Row 3: Ch 2, hdc2tog over next 2 sts, hdc across to last 3 sts, hdc2tog over next 2 sts, hdc in last st—30 sts, turn.

Rep Rows 2 and 3 until 6 sts remain, turn. Do not fasten off.

Buttonhole:

Row 1: Ch 1, sc in each st across, turn—6 sc.

Row 2: Ch 1, sc in next 2 sc, ch 2, sk next 2 sc, sc in last 2 sc, turn—4 sc, 1 ch-2 sp.

Row 3: Ch 1, sc in next 2 sc, 2 sc in ch-2 space, sc in last 2 sc—6 sc. Fasten off.

Rep edging and buttonhole for opposite side edge.

ATTACH MAIN BODY AND ARM WRAP

Lay main body flat front side down, matching buckle openings. Mark center back at top edge of main body and center of long edge of arm wrap and pin tog. Pin center with right sides together. Beg pinning right sides of edges together, working out from each side of center, until body piece is connected evenly and ending at each side of main body. Join yarn and work sl st evenly along to join edges. Fasten off.

Hood

With G/6 (4 mm) hook and RS of back arm wrap facing, count to the 14th "V" eyelet of the arm wrap and attach yarn to edge.

Row 1: Ch 1, sc in first eyelet, *sc in leg (star point), sc in eyelet; rep from * across, turn—34 sts.

Row 2: Ch 2 (counts as hdc), hdc in each sc across, turn.

Row 3: Ch 1, *dc in next hdc, sl st in next hdc; rep from * across, turn.

Rep Rows 2 and 3 for a total of 24 rows (or desired length). Do not fasten off.

Fold edge of last row worked in half, RS tog and sl st edges tog beg from outer edge to corner to form hood. Fasten off.

Finishing

Buttons: Lay swaddle flat with front side up. Place each button 3" (7.5 cm) down from top edge of sack and ¾" (2 cm) from side and sew in place to each side.

Ribbon: Lay swaddle flat with front side up. Beginning at center bottom right (or left) eyelet, weave ribbon under and over alternating eyelets around, returning to beginning at opposite front eyelet.

Weave in ends.

Ladybug the Dachshund

SWEATER

DESIGNED BY BRENDA K. B. ANDERSON

At her last birthday, designer Brenda Anderson's dachshund friend, Ladybug, received a little doggie sweater, which she wore proudly for the rest of the party (even though it wasn't nearly long enough for her extra-long torso). It was so cute it inspired Brenda to stitch up an appliqué wiener dog to dress up a classic cardigan.

FINISHED SIZE
Instructions are written for size Newborn. Changes for 3 months, 6 months, 12 months, 18 months, and 24 months are in parentheses.

Chest circumference: 19 (19¾, 20½, 21¼, 21¾, 22½)" (48.5 [50, 52, 54, 55, 57] cm).

Shown in size 18 months.

YARN
Fingering weight (#1 Super Fine).

Shown here: Berroco Ultra Alpaca Fine (50% superwash wool, 30% nylon, 20% superfine alpaca; 433 yd [400 m]/3½ oz [100 g]): #12178 grapefruit mix (MC), 2 skeins; #1214 steel cut oats (CC), 1 skein.

HOOK
Size C/2 (2.75 mm). *Adjust hook size if necessary to obtain correct gauge.*

NOTIONS
Stitch markers (m); yarn needle; 1 skein dark brown embroidery floss; 2 pieces ⅝" (1.5 cm)-wide ribbon, cut to length of sweater front opening plus 1" (2.5 cm); 4–6 sew-on size 3 snaps; 4–6 buttons with ½" (1.3 cm) diameter; sewing needle and thread.

GAUGE
23 sts and 14½ rows = 4" (10 cm) in dc worked in turned rows.

23 sts = 4" (10 cm) in hdc for trim and button/snap edging (row gauge of hdc is not crucial).

NOTES
Sweater is worked in one piece from the top down. Yoke is worked first in turned rows, sts are set aside for sleeves, then body is worked in turned rows. Button/snap edging is worked sideways along front edges. Sleeves are worked in joined, turned rows. Dachshund appliqué is stitched on later.

Turning ch do not count as sts.

STITCH GUIDE

Esc3tog (extended single crochet 3 stitches together): Insert hook in next st, yo and pull up lp, yo and draw through 1 lp, [insert hook in following st, yo and pull up lp, yo and draw through 1 lp] twice, yo and draw through all 4 lps.

Scbb (single crochet through back bar) [worked in the round]: This is just a regular sc st made into the back bar of the previous rnd of hdc sts. The back bar is the horizontal dash on WS of a hdc st situated about half-way between top and bottom of st. When working in this st, slide hook through bar from top to bottom in a downward motion.

Yoke

With MC, ch 87 sts.

Row 1: (WS) [Dc, ch 1, dc] in 4th ch from hook, dc in next 16 ch, [dc, ch 1, dc] in next ch, dc in next 26 ch, [dc, ch 1, dc] in next ch, dc in next 16 ch, [dc, ch 1, dc] in next ch, dc in next 22 ch—92 sts.

Row 2: (RS) Ch 3 (does not count as st now and throughout), turn, *dc in each dc to next ch-1 sp, [dc, ch 1, dc] in next ch-sp, rep from * 3 more times, dc in last st—100 sts.

Row 3: Ch 3, turn, dc in next 2 sts, *[dc, ch 1, dc] in next ch-1 sp, dc in each dc ending at next ch-1 sp, rep from * twice more, [dc, ch 1, dc] in next ch-1 sp, dc in each st to end—108 sts.

Rows 4–12 (4–13, 4–14, 4–15, 4–16, 4–17): Continue working in turned rows, making 1 dc in each dc st across

and [dc, ch-1, dc] in each of the 4 ch-1 sps across row. If you have trouble spotting the ch-1 sps, place a marker (pm) in each one—180 (188, 196, 204, 212, 220) sts.

Sizes Newborn (6 Months, 18 Months) only

Row 13 (15, 17): (WS) Ch 3, turn, dc in next 12 (14, 16) sts, [dc, ch 1, dc] in next ch-1 sp, dc in next 40 (44, 48) sts, [dc, ch 1, dc] in next ch-1 sp, dc in next 50 (54, 58) sts, [dc, ch 1, dc] in next ch-1 sp, dc in next 40 (44, 48) sts, [dc, ch 1, dc] in next ch-1 sp, dc in next 34 (36, 38) sts—188 (204, 220) sts. Do not fasten off.

Divide for Arms for Sizes Newborn (6 Months, 18 Months) only

Row 14 (16, 18): (RS) Ch 3, turn, dc in next 35 (37, 39) sts, dc in next ch-1 sp, pm in same ch-1 sp, sk all dc sts to next ch-1 sp, dc in ch-1 sp, dc in next 52 (56, 60) sts, dc in next ch-1 sp, pm

in this same ch-1 sp, sk all dc to next ch-1 sp, dc in ch-1 sp, dc in last 13 (15, 17) sts—104 (112, 120) sts, not including armhole sts.

Sizes 3 (12, 24) Months only

Row 14 (16, 18): (RS) Ch 3, turn, dc in next 35 (37, 39) sts, [dc, ch 1, dc] in next ch-1 sp, dc in next 42 (46, 50) sts, [dc, ch 1, dc] in next ch-1 sp, dc in next 52 (56, 60) sts, [dc, ch 1, dc] in next ch-1 sp, dc in next 42 (46, 50) sts, [dc, ch 1, dc] in next ch-1 sp, dc in next 13 (15, 17) sts—196 (212, 228) sts. Do not fasten off.

Divide for Arms for Sizes 3 (12, 24) Months only

Row 15 (17, 19): (WS) Ch 3, turn, dc in next 14 (16, 18) sts, dc in next ch-1 sp, pm in same ch-1 sp, sk all dc sts to next ch-1 sp, dc in ch-1 sp, dc in next 54 (58, 62) sts, dc in next ch-1 sp, pm in same ch-1 sp, sk all dc sts to next ch-1 sp, dc in ch-1 sp, dc in last 36 (38,

40) sts—108 (116, 124) sts, not including armhole sts

Body

Rows 15–32 (16–34, 17–36, 18–38, 19–40, 20–42): Ch 3, turn, dc in each st across—104 (108, 112, 116, 120, 124) sts. Row 32 (34, 36, 38, 40, 42) is a RS row.

After working last row, keeping RS facing, do not turn, but rotate to work up the right front opening as follows:

Row 1: (RS) Using st markers, divide right front edge into 4 equal sections. Ch 2 (does not count as st), hdc 13 (14, 14, 15, 16, 17) in each section—52 (56, 56, 60, 64, 68) hdc sts evenly spaced along edge.

Rows 3–4. Ch 2, turn, hdc in each st. Fasten off.

Join yarn to top corner of left front opening by pulling up a lp, rep Rows 1–4 above to create left front button edging. Fasten off.

Sleeve (make 2)

Note: Sizes Newborn, 6 months, and 18 months beg with RS facing; sizes 3 months, 12 months, and 24 months beg with WS facing.

Rnd 1: Pull up MC yarn from marked ch-1 sp at underarm, ch 3 (does not count as st), dc in same ch-1 sp, dc in next 42 (44, 46, 48, 50, 52) sts, dc in next ch-1 sp, sl st to first dc of rnd to join—44 (46, 48, 50, 52, 54) sts.

Rnd 2: Ch 3, turn, dc around, join.

Rnd 3: Ch 3, turn, dc2tog (see Glossary), dc in next 40 (42, 44, 46, 48, 50) sts, dc2tog, join—42 (44, 46, 48, 50, 52) sts.

Rnds 4–6: Ch 3, turn, dc in each st around, join.

Rnd 7: Ch 3, turn, dc2tog, dc in next 38 (40, 42, 44, 46, 48) sts, dc2tog, join—40 (42, 44, 46, 48, 50) sts.

Rnds 8–10: Ch 3, turn, dc in each st around, join.

Rnd 11: Ch 3, turn, dc2tog, dc in next 36 (38, 40, 42, 44, 46) sts, dc2tog, join—38 (40, 42, 44, 46, 48) sts.

Rnds 12–14: Ch 3, turn, dc in each st around, join.

Rnd 15: Ch 3, turn, dc2tog, dc in next 34 (36, 38, 40, 42, 44) sts, dc2tog, join—36 (38, 40, 42, 44, 46) sts.

Rnds 16–18: Ch 3, turn, dc in each st around, join.

Rnd 19: Ch 3, turn, dc2tog, dc in next 32 (34, 36, 38, 40, 42) sts, dc2tog, join—34 (36, 38, 40, 42, 44) sts.

Rnd(s) 20 (20–21, 20–22, 20–23, 20–22, 20–22): Ch 3, turn, dc in each st around, join.

Sizes Newborn, 3 Months, 6 Months, and 12 Months only
Fasten off.

Sizes 18 (24) Months only
Rnd 23: Ch 3, turn, dc2tog, dc in next 38 (40) sts, dc2tog, join—40 (42) sts.

9½ (10, 10½, 11, 11½, 13)"
24 (25.5, 26.5, 28, 29, 33) cm

4½"
11.5 cm

2¾"
7 cm

8 (8¼, 8¾, 9, 9½, 9¾)"
20.5 (21, 22, 23, 24, 25) cm

6¼ (6½, 7, 7¼, 7¼, 7½)"
16 (16.5, 18, 18.5, 18.5, 19) cm

9½ (10, 10½, 11, 11½, 12)"
24 (25.5, 26.5, 28, 29, 30.5) cm

6 (6¼, 6½, 6¾, 7, 8¼)"
15 (16, 16.5, 17, 18, 21) cm

3¾ (4, 4¼, 4½, 4¾, 5)"
9.5 (10, 11, 11.5, 12, 12.5) cm

1" (2.5) cm

18 (18¾, 19½, 20¼, 20¾, 21½)"
45.5 (47.5, 49.5, 51.5, 52.5, 54.5) cm

Note: Measurements given exclude ¼" (6 mm) edging or button/snap edging.

Rnds 24 (24–29): Ch 3, turn, dc around, join. Fasten off.

SLEEVE EDGING (WORKED SAME FOR EACH SLEEVE)

With RS facing, join CC in last st of previous rnd by pulling up a lp.

Rnd 1: Ch 1, hdc evenly around, do not join—34 (36, 38, 40, 40, 42) sts.

Rnd 2: Scbb (see Stitch Guide) around. Fasten off.

Body Edging

Rnd 1: With RS facing pull up lp of CC in hdc at bottom corner of right front opening. Ch 2, 3 hdc in same corner stitch, hdc in each st along right front opening until one st remains, 3 hdc in last st, rotate to work along neckline as follows: 5 hdc evenly spaced along top edge of button/snap edging, hdc in each st of beg ch along neck edge, 5 hdc sts evenly spaced along top edge of button/snap edging for other side of opening, 3 hdc in first hdc of left front opening, hdc in each st along front opening to last st, 3 hdc in last st, rotate to work along bottom edge of sweater as follows: 5 hdc evenly spaced along side edge of button/snap edging, hdc in each st across bottom edge of sweater, 5 hdc evenly spaced across bottom edge of button/snap edging, do not join.

Rnd 2: Scbb in each st around entire edge. Fasten off.

Dachshund Appliqué

With CC, ch 93 (97, 101, 105, 109, 113) sts.

Rnd 1: 2 sc in 2nd ch from hook (first ch from hook does not count as st), pm in first sc of rnd to keep track of beg of rnds, sc in each st until 11 sts remain, sc3tog (see Glossary), pm in sc3tog, sc in next 7 sts, 2 sc in last st, rotate to work in opposite side of ch, 2 sc in next st, sc in next 8 sts, 3 sc in next st, pm in center of these 3 sts, sc in each st to last st, 2 sc in last st. Do not join.

Rnd 2: Rotate work to continue working in the rnd (beg with marked st), 2 sc in next 2 sts, sc in each st to next m, sc in marked st (replace m), sl st blo in next 4 sts, sc in next 3 sts, 2 sc in next 4 sts, sc in next 3 sts, sl st blo in next 4 sts, sc in next 2 sts, sc in marked st (replace m), sc in each st to last 2 sts, 2 sc in each of the last 2 sts.

Rnd 3: [Sc in next st, 2 sc in next st] twice, sc in each st to one st before the next marked st, sc3tog, sl st blo in next 4 sts, sc in next 2 sts, [2 sc in next st, sc in next st] twice, [sc in next st, 2 sc in next st] twice, sc in next 2 sts, sl st blo in next 4 sts, sc in next 3 sts, 3 sc in marked st (replace m in middle of 3 sc), sc in each st to last 4 sts remain, [2 sc in next st, sc in next st] twice.

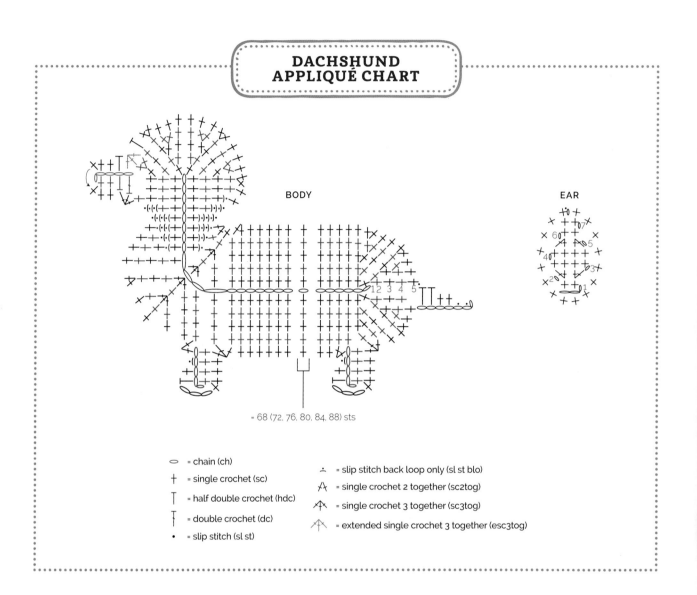

DACHSHUND APPLIQUÉ CHART

BODY

EAR

= 68 (72, 76, 80, 84, 88) sts

◯ = chain (ch)

+ = single crochet (sc)

T = half double crochet (hdc)

‡ = double crochet (dc)

• = slip stitch (sl st)

⊥ = slip stitch back loop only (sl st blo)

⋏ = single crochet 2 together (sc2tog)

⋏ = single crochet 3 together (sc3tog)

⋏ = extended single crochet 3 together (esc3tog)

Rnd 4: Sc in next st, 2 sc in next st, sc in next 2 sts, 2 sc in next st, sc in each st to next m, sc in marked st (replace m in new st), sc in next st, sl st blo in next 4 sts, sc in next 2 sts, [2 sc in next st, sc in next 2 sts] 3 times, 2 sc in next st, ch 5, sc in bottom of 2nd ch from hook (first ch does not count as st), sc in next ch, hdc in next ch, dc in next ch, sk next 2 sts of Rnd 3, sc in next st, sl st blo in next 3 sts, sc in next 5 sts, sc in marked st (replace m in new st), sc in next 3 sts, ch 5, sc in bottom of 2nd ch from hook, sc in next 3 ch, sc in next st of Rnd 3, sc in each st to last 6 sts, ch 5, sc in bottom of 2nd ch from

hook, sc in next 3 ch, sc in next st of Rnd 3, sc in next 3 sts, 2 sc in next st, sc in last st.

Rnd 5: Sc in next 3 sts, 2 sc in next st, sc in next 2 sts, 2 sc in next st, sc in each st to 2 sts before next marked st, sc2tog (see Glossary), sc in marked st, sc2tog, sl st blo in next 2 sts, sc in next 2 sts, 2 sc in next st, sc in next 3 sts, 2 sc in next st, sc in next 6 sts, 2 sc in next st, hdc in next st, esc3tog (see Stitch Guide), hdc in next st, sc in next st, 2 sc in next st, rotate to work around other side of nose, 2 sc in next st, sc in next st, sc3tog, sl st blo in next

2 sts, sc in next 4 sts, 2 sc in next st, sc in next 4 sts, sc2tog, sl st blo in next st, sc in next st, hdc in next st, ch 3, rotate to work around other side of leg, 2 sc in next st, sc in next 2 sts, sc3tog, sc in each st to last st before next leg, sc2tog, sl st blo in next st, 1 sc in next st, hdc in next st, ch 3, rotate to work around other side of leg, 2 sc in next sc st, sc in next 2 sts, sc3tog, sc in next st, 2 sc in next st, sc in next 2 sts, ch 7, sl st in bottom of 2nd ch from hook, sl st in next ch, sc in next 2 sts, hdc in next 2 sts, sk last st, sl st in first st of rnd to join. Fasten off with long yarn tail for sewing.

EDGING

Using brown embroidery floss, pull up lp from the blo of first st of rnd, sl st blo in each st all the way around edge of dachshund appliqué. Make sts loose enough so as not to constrict the edges of appliqué.

EAR

Row 1: Using CC, ch 3, sc in bottom of 2nd ch from hook (first ch from hook does not count as st), sc in next st—2 sts.

Row 2: Ch 1, turn, 2 sc in each st—4 sts.

Rows 3 and 4: Ch 1, turn, sc in each st—4 sts.

Row 5: Ch 1, turn, sc2tog twice—2 sts.

Rows 6 and 7: Ch 1, turn, sc in each st—2 sts. Do not fasten off.

EDGING

Ch 1, keeping same side facing, rotate ear and 16 sc evenly spaced along side edges around ear, ending at top of other side edge of ear. Fasten off, leaving tail for sewing. Using brown embroidery floss, pull up lp in blo of first sc of edging, Sl st blo in each sc around ear—16 sts. Fasten off.

Finishing

Block sweater and appliqué. Use yarn tails where arms were added to close small holes in underarm. Weave in all ends except for CC yarn tail for sewing appliqué. Pin ribbon to underlap/overlap of button/snap edging. Tuck ½" (1.3 cm) under on each end of ribbon. Using sewing needle and thread, whipstitch (see Glossary) edges of ribbon to sweater using a small st. Sew buttons to front of sweater; make sure they are evenly spaced before sew-ing them on. Sew male side of snaps directly behind the buttons, and sew female side of snaps to match place-ment. Pin appliqué to sweater, making sure that it is neither constricting, nor stretching out the sweater. Using CC yarn tail (and/or additional CC yarn), sew edges of appliqué to sweater using a backstitch (see Glossary) next to the embroidery-floss edging. Sew ear to head using CC yarn tails. Using brown embroidery floss, ch 3, then fasten off. Sew this tiny chain to dog's face in a curved line for mouth. Using embroidery floss and yarn needle, make a large French knot (see Glos-sary) for the dog's eye.

Finley the Fox

BIB

DESIGNED BY LISA VAN KLAVEREN

This foxy design is based on some gorgeous handmade fabric bibs that designer Lisa van Klaveren had for her girls when they were little. The adjustable neckline allows baby to keep wearing it as he grows!

FINISHED SIZE

This bib features a ribbed collar with adjustable button closure at the back, so it will fit a little baby or an older toddler.

Width: About 8" (20.5 cm).

YARN

Worsted weight (#4 Medium).

Shown here: Blue Sky Alpacas Worsted Cotton (100% cotton; 150 yd [137 m]/3½ oz [100 g]): #622 pumpkin (A), #80 bone (B), and #623 toffee (C), 1 skein each.

HOOK

Size H/8 (5 mm). *Adjust hook size if necessary to obtain correct gauge.*

NOTIONS

Two ½" (13 mm) buttons; yarn needle; sewing needle; sewing thread.

GAUGE

15 sts and 18 rows = 4" (10 cm) in patt st.

Upper Bib

RIBBED YOKE

Row 1: Beg at neckline, ch 57 with (A), sc in 2nd ch from hook and in each ch across, turn—56 sts.

Row 2: Ch 1, *sc blo in next 13 sc, 2 sc blo in next sc; rep from * across, turn—60 sts.

Row 3: Ch 1, *sc blo in next 14 sc, 2 sc blo in next sc; rep from * across, turn—64 sts.

Row 4: (buttonhole) Ch 1, sc blo in next 2 sc, ch 1, sk next sc (first buttonhole), sc blo in next 6 sc, ch 1, sk next sc (2nd buttonhole), sc blo in next 5 sc, 2 sc blo in next sc, *sc blo in next 15 sc, 2 sc blo in next sc; rep from * across, turn—68 sc, 2 ch-1 buttonholes.

Row 5: Ch 1, *sc blo in next 16 sts, 2 sc blo in next st; rep from * across, turn—72 sc.

Row 6: Ch 1, *sc blo in next 17 sc, 2 sc blo in next sc; rep from * across, turn—76 sc.

Row 7: Ch 1, *sc blo in next 18 sc, 2 sc blo in next sc; rep from * across—80 sc. Fasten off.

LOWER BIB

Row 8: Sk first 20 sc of Row 7 of collar and join (A) with sc blo in next sc, sc2tog in blo, sc blo in next 16 sc, [2 sc blo in next sc] twice, sc blo in next 16 sc, sc2tog in blo, sc blo in next sc, leave rem sts unworked, turn—40 sts.

Row 9: Ch 1, sc blo in first sc, sc2tog in blo, sc blo in next 16 sc, [2 sc blo in next sc] twice, sc blo in next 16 sc, sc2tog in blo, sc blo in last sc, turn.

Rows 10–19: Rep Row 9, joining (B) in last sc of Row 19. Fasten off (A).

Row 20–26: With (B), rep Row 9. Fasten off.

Eye (make 2)

With (C), make an adjustable ring (see Glossary). Ch 1, 6 sc in ring—6 sts. Fasten off, leaving long tail to attach eye to bib.

Nose

Rnd 1: With (C), make an adjustable ring. Ch 1, 6 sc in ring—6 sc.

Rnd 2: [Sc in next sc, 2 sc in next sc] 3 times—9 sts.

Fasten off leaving tail to attach nose to bib.

Finishing

Weave in ends.

BUTTONS

Place first button on center of collar buttonband, ¾" (2 cm) from edge, and sew in place. Sew second button 1¾" (4.5 cm) from first button.

EYES AND NOSE

Sew eyes and nose to front of bib. Refer to photos for help with placement.

Eddy
BURP CLOTHS

DESIGNED BY BRENDA K. B. ANDERSON

The peanut shape of these burp cloths is cleverly designed to sit nicely over your shoulder as you hold baby. The swirl effect is both for aesthetics and in hopes that it will hypnotize the little one into a nice after-dinner snooze.

FINISHED SIZE
Each cloth measures about 8½" (21.5 cm) wide and 16" (40.5 cm) long.

YARN
Fingering weight (#1 Super Fine).

Shown here: Brown Sheep Company Cotton Fine (80% cotton, 20% merino; 222 yd [203 m]/1¾ oz [50 g]):

For Burp Cloths 1 and 2: #CF625 terracotta canyon, #CF100 cotton ball, and #CF825 truffle, 1 skein each.

For Burp Cloths 3 and 4: #CF825 truffle, #CF640 spryte, and #CF120 honey butter, 1 skein each.

Note: Only 1 skein is needed of each of the 3 different colors of your choice to make 3 burp cloths. See notes below for further information.

HOOK
Size C/2 (2.75 mm). *Adjust hook size if necessary to obtain correct gauge.*

NOTIONS
Stitch markers, one in contrasting color (m); yarn bobbin for color D (optional); yarn needle.

GAUGE
To make gauge swatch, work through Rnd 5 of Spiral Motif #1 instructions; piece should measure about 3¾" (9.5 cm) from corner to corner.

Note: Obtaining the suggested gauge will help ensure that burp cloth ends up a good size and has a nice density without being too stiff. However, getting gauge is not crucial, as long as you like the way the fabric looks and feels, and you don't mind if the cloth is a bit smaller or larger than shown.

NOTES
There are 4 working lps at all times when creating the spiral motif.

Work one color for specified sts, then insert hook into next working lp of next color and work for specified sts, and so forth, taking turns, working a little at a time for each color.

Colors C and D are made with 2 separate balls of the same color (they are always the same color). There is no need to buy a separate skein for color D; use yarn bobbin or wind up a 2" (5 cm) diameter ball from skein of color C and use as "color D."

Each burp cloth is made of 2 motifs that are sewn tog. Each motif is made in the same way; the only difference is the order of colors A and B. In Motif #1, beg with color A and switch to color B. In Motif #2, beg with color B and switch to color A.

Each burp cloth requires one each of Spiral Motif #1 and Spiral Motif #2.

Colorways: See Colorways sidebar (page 86) and chart (page 87).

COLORWAYS

Burp Cloth 1: Truffle as color A, cotton ball as color B, and terracotta canyon as colors C and D.

Burp Cloth 2: Terracotta canyon as color A, cotton ball as color B, and truffle as colors C and D.

Burp Cloth 3: Truffle as color A, honey butter as color B, and spryte as colors C and D.

Burp Cloth 4: Spryte as color A, truffle as color B, and honey butter as colors C and D.

Spiral Motif #1

Prep: Wind 2nd color D (see notes).

Rnd 1: (RS) (set-up spiral) Using A, make an adjustable ring (see Glossary), ch 1, *[sc, hdc, dc] in ring, elongate working lp of last st completed so that it will not ravel**, remove hook from lp, insert hook in same lp, yo with B and bring up lp, ch 1, rep from * to **, remove hook from lp, insert hook in same lp, yo with C and pull up lp, ch 1, rep from * to **, remove hook from lp, insert hook in same lp, yo with D and pull up lp, ch 1, [sc, hdc, dc] in 2nd ch from hook. Do not elongate lp or remove hook. Pull on tail end of A to tighten ring—12 sts.

Rnd 2: Continuing with D, 2 dc in each of next 3 sts, place marker (pm) in first st made to keep track of beg of rnds, elongate lp, remove hook from lp, place hook in A lp from st below (pull on A yarn tail to shorten lp back to normal), 2 dc in next 3 sts, elongate lp, remove hook from lp, place hook in B lp from st below (pull on yarn tail to shorten lp back to normal), 2 dc in each of next 3 sts, elongate lp, remove hook from lp, place hook in C lp from st below (pull on yarn tail to shorten lp back to normal), 2 dc in each of next 3 sts, do not elongate lp or remove hook from lp—24 sts.

Note: The beg rnd marker does not signify a change in color, but merely the beg of rnd. Only change color when directed to move to next available working lp.

COLORWAYS

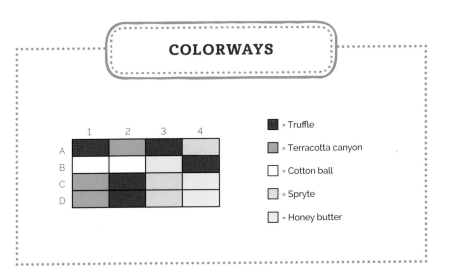

	1	2	3	4
A				
B				
C				
D				

■ = Truffle

■ = Terracotta canyon

□ = Cotton ball

□ = Spryte

□ = Honey butter

Rnd 3: Continuing with C, [dc in next st, 2 dc in next st] 3 times, elongate lp, remove hook from lp, place hook in D lp from st below (pull on yarn tail to shorten lp back to normal), [dc in next st, 2 dc in next st] 3 times, elongate lp, remove hook from lp, place hook in A lp from st below (pull on yarn tail to shorten lp back to normal), [dc in next st, 2 dc in next st] 3 times, elongate lp, remove hook from lp, place hook in B lp from st below (pull on yarn tail to shorten lp back to normal), [dc in next st, 2 dc in next st] 3 times, do not elongate lp or remove hook from lp—36 sts.

Rnd 4: Continuing with B, [dc in next 2 sts, 2 dc in next st] 3 times, elongate lp, remove hook from lp, place hook in C lp from st below (pull on yarn tail to shorten lp back to normal), [dc in next 2 sts, 2 dc in next st] 3 times, elongate lp, remove hook from lp, place hook in D lp from st below (pull on yarn tail to shorten lp back to normal), [dc in next 2 sts, 2 dc in next st] 3 times, elongate lp, remove hook from lp, place hook in A lp from st below (pull on A yarn tail to shorten lp back to normal), [dc in next 2 sts, 2 dc in next st] 3 times, do not elongate lp or remove hook from lp—48 sts.

Rnd 5: Continue with same color, *[dc in next 3 sts, 2 dc in next st] 3 times, change to next lp**, rep from * to ** twice more, [dc in next 3 sts, 2 dc in next st] 3 times, do not change color—60 sts.

Rnd 6: Continue with same color, *[dc in next 4 sts, 2 dc in next st] 3 times, change to next lp**, rep from * to ** twice more, [dc in next 4 sts, 2 dc in next st] 3 times, do not change color—72 sts.

Rnd 7: Continue with same color, *[dc in next 5 sts, 2 dc in next st] 3 times, change to next lp**, rep from * to ** twice more, [dc in next 5 sts, 2 dc in next st] 3 times, do not change color—84 sts.

Rnd 8: Continue with same color, *[dc in next 6 sts, 2 dc in next st] 3 times, change to next lp**, rep from * to ** twice more, [dc in next 6 sts, 2 dc in next st] 3 times, do not change color—96 sts.

Rnd 9: Continue with same color, *[dc in next 7 sts, 2 dc in next st] 3 times, change to next lp**, rep from * to ** twice more, [dc in next 7 sts, 2 dc in next st] 3 times, do not change color—108 sts.

Rnd 10: Continue with same color, *[dc in next 8 sts, 2 dc in next st] 3 times, change to next lp**, rep from * to ** twice more, [dc in next 8 sts, 2 dc in next st] 3 times, do not change color—120 sts. Fasten off, leaving long tail for sewing.

FINISHING SPIRAL MOTIF #1
Bring all other working lps to end at same point (just above last st of color C) as follows:

Insert hook in working lp of color B, [dc in next 9 sts, 2 dc in next st] 3 times. Fasten off, leaving long tail for sewing.

Insert hook in working lp of color A, [dc in next 9 sts, 2 dc in next st] 3 times, (dc in next 10 dc, 2 dc in next st) 3 times. Fasten off, leaving long tail for sewing.

Insert hook in working lp of color D, [dc into each of the next 9 sts, 2 dc into the next st] 3 times, [dc in next 10 dc, 2 dc in next st] 3 times, [dc in next 11 sts, 2 dc in next st] 3 times. Fasten off, leaving long tail for sewing. Pm in 11th st from end (for beg of gusset) and pm in contrasting color in 13th st from end (indicates where to join yarn for last dc rnd).

Gusset Spiral Motif #1
With RS facing, pull up lp of color C in marked st, ch 3 (does not count as st), beg with same st, tr in next 2 sts, dc in next 2 sts, hdc in next 2 sts, sc in next 2 sts, sl st in next st. Fasten off, leaving last 2 sts unworked. Set aside.

Spiral Motif #2
Prep: Wind 2nd color D (see notes).

Rnd 1: (set-up spiral) Using color B, make an adjustable ring, ch 1, *[sc, hdc, dc] in ring, elongate working lp as for Spiral Motif 1**, remove hook from lp, insert hook in same lp, yo with A and pull up lp, ch 1, rep from * to **, remove hook from lp, insert hook in same lp, yo with C and pull up lp, ch 1, rep from * to **, remove hook from lp, insert hook in same lp, yo with D and pull up lp, ch 1, [sc, hdc, dc] in 2nd ch from hook, do not elongate lp or remove hook from lp—12 sts. Gently pull on tail end of B to close together center of adjustable ring.

Rnd 2: Continuing with D, 2 dc in each of next 3 sts, pm in first st made to keep track of beg of the rnds, elongate lp, remove hook from lp, place hook in B lp from st below (pull yarn tail to shorten lp back to normal), 2 dc in next 3 sts, elongate lp, remove hook from lp, place hook in A lp from st below (pull on yarn tail to shorten lp back to normal), 2 dc in each of next 3 sts, elongate lp, remove hook from lp, place hook in C lp from st below (pull on yarn tail to shorten lp back to normal), 2 dc in each of next 3 sts, do not elongate lp or remove hook from lp—24 sts.

Note: The beg rnd marker does not signify a change in color, but merely the beg of rnd. Only change color when directed to move to next available working lp.

Rnd 3: Continuing with C, [dc in next st, 2 dc in next st] 3 times, elongate lp, remove hook from lp, place hook in D lp from st below (pull on yarn tail to shorten lp back to normal), [dc in next st, 2 dc in next st] 3 times, elongate lp, remove hook from lp, place hook in B lp from st below (pull on yarn tail to shorten lp back to normal), [dc in next st, 2 dc in next st] 3 times, elongate lp, remove hook from lp, place hook in A lp from st below (pull on yarn tail to shorten lp back to normal), [dc in next st, 2 dc in next st] 3 times, do not elongate lp or remove hook from lp—36 sts.

Rnd 4: Continuing with A, [dc in next 2 sts, 2 dc in next st] 3 times, elongate lp, remove hook from lp, place hook in C lp from st below (pull on yarn tail to shorten lp back to normal), [dc in next 2 sts, 2 dc in next st] 3 times, elongate lp, remove hook from lp, place hook in D lp from st below (pull on yarn tail to shorten lp back to normal), [dc in next 2 sts, 2 dc in next st] 3 times, elongate lp, remove hook from lp, place hook in

B loop from st below (pull on B yarn tail to shorten lp back to normal), [dc in next 2 sts, 2 dc in next st] 3 times, do not elongate lp or remove hook from loop—48 sts.

Work Rnds 5-10 same as for Spiral Motif #1 in color sequence as est.

FINISHING SPIRAL MOTIF #2
Bring all other working lps to end at same point (just above last st of color C) as follows:

Insert hook in working lp of color A, [dc in next 9 sts, 2 dc in next st] 3 times. Fasten off, leaving long tail for sewing.

Insert hook in working lp of color B, [dc in next 9 sts, 2 dc in next st] 3 times, [dc in next 10 dc, 2 dc in next st] 3 times. Fasten off, leaving long tail for sewing.

Insert hook in working lp of color D, [dc in next 9 sts, 2 dc in next st] 3 times, [dc in next 10 dc, 2 dc in next st] 3 times, [dc in next 11 sts, 2 dc in next st] 3 times. Fasten off, leaving long tail for sewing. Pm in 11th st from end (indicates beg of gusset).

Gusset Spiral Motif #2
Work gusset same as for Spiral Motif #1.

Attaching Motifs
Motifs fit together like a puzzle; stripes should continue from one

motif to the next. Sew motifs together using yarn tails in matching colors. Sew the top edge of the gusset to opposite motif to fill in the gap between motifs.

Final Rnd
Rnd 1: With RS facing and using color C, yo and pull up yarn from st with contrast m. Ch 3 (does not count as st), dc in same st, *beg with next st, dc3tog (see Glossary) making last two legs of dec inside edge of gusset. When stitching inside edge of gusset, place sts along post of first tr, *not* in the ch-3 turning ch. Last leg of dec should be about halfway up side edge of gusset. Work another dc3tog with first 2 legs of dec made in the side edge of gusset and 3rd leg of decrease in first available st of next motif. Dc in each of the sts around edge of motif except at an inc st. Dc in first dc of inc, 2 dc in 2nd dc of inc. Continue around to last st of this motif. Rep from * all the way around both motifs, sl st in first dc of rnd to join.

Rnd 2: Work 1 complete rnd of rev sc (see Glossary). Make sure that rev sc does not stretch out edge of burp cloth. If this starts to happen, use a smaller hook size. Sl st to fasten off.

Finishing
Weave in ends. Block.

Spike the Hedgehog
HAT

DESIGNED BY BRENDA K. B. ANDERSON

What's even cuter than a hedgehog? A baby in a hedgehog hat. Babies don't always appreciate the warming benefits of hats, but you won't have any trouble getting yours to wear this adorable and fun-to-make topper.

FINISHED SIZE

Instructions are written for size 6-12 months. Changes for 12-18 months and 18-24 months are in parentheses.

Circumference: 15 (16½, 18)" (38 [42, 45.5] cm).

Shown in size 18-24 months.

YARN

Worsted weight (#4 Medium).

Shown here: Lion Brand Heartland (100% acrylic; 251 yd [230 m]/5 oz [142 g]): #098 Acadia (MC), #122 Grand Canyon (CC1), and #125 Mammoth Cave (CC2), 1 skein each.

HOOK

Size H/8 (5 mm). *Adjust hook size if necessary to obtain correct gauge.*

NOTIONS

Stitch markers (m); yarn needle; small amount of polyester stuffing for nose; 2 flat white ⅞"" (22 mm) buttons (for eyes); 2 flat black ⅝"" (15 mm) buttons (for eyes); sewing needle and black thread; black embroidery floss; embroidery needle.

GAUGE

16 sts and 19 rounds = 4" (10 cm) in sc worked in the rnd. To make a gauge swatch, work Rnds 1-8 of hat instructions; circle measures about 4" (10 cm) in diameter.

NOTES

Hat is worked in the rnd from the top down. Face, muzzle, ears, and coat are made separately and stitched to hat. Coat base is worked separately beg in the rnd at top of head and switching to turned rows to work down back of head. After working edging around perimeter of coat, hairs are added to coat.

When making coat base, pay close attention to whether sts are to be worked under blo or flo. Unused lps should all be on RS of coat base and will be used later when hairs are added.

Eyes are stacks of buttons sewn to hat. Nose and mouth are embroidered.

STITCH GUIDE

Hs (hair stitch): Ch 5, beg in 2nd ch from hook and working in bottom ridge lp of ch, sl st in next 4 ch—*1 Hs made.*

Bottom Ridge Loop of a Chain Stitch: This is the part of the chain stitch that is *opposite* the 2 lps (the ones that form the V) that you would normally insert your hook under. In other words, if you turn the chain upside down so that you are looking at the bottom of it, you will see a line of dashes. It is under each dash that you would insert your hook if you were instructed to crochet into the bottom of each chain stitch.

Hat

Rnd 1: With MC make an adjustable ring, 6 sc in ring. Pull on beg tail to tighten ring—6 sts. Place marker (pm) to keep track of beg of rnds.

Rnd 2: 2 sc in each st around—12 sts.

Rnd 3: [2 sc in next st, sc in next st] 6 times—18 sts.

Rnd 4: [Sc in next st, 2 sc in next st, sc in next st] 6 times—24 sts.

Rnd 5: [Sc in next 3 sts, 2 sc in next st] 6 times—30 sts.

Rnd 6: [2 sc in next st, sc in next 4 sts] 6 times—36 sts.

Rnd 7: [Sc in next 2 sts, 2 sc in next st, sc in next 3 sts] 6 times—42 sts.

Rnd 8: [Sc in next 4 sts, 2 sc in next st, sc in next 2 sts] 6 times—48 sts.

Sizes Medium and Large only
Rnd 9: [Sc in next 7 sts, 2 sc in next st] 6 times—54 sts.

Size Large only
Rnd 10: [Sc in next 4 sts, 2 sc in next st, sc in next 4 sts] 6 times—60 sts.

All Sizes
Rnd 9 (10, 11): [Sc in next 15 (17, 19) sts, 2 sc in next st] 3 times—51 (57, 63) sts.

Rnd 10 (11, 12): [Sc in next 5 (6, 7) sts, 2 sc in next st, sc in next 11 (12, 13) sts] 3 times—54 (60, 66) sts.

Rnd 11 (12, 13): [Sc in next 13 (14, 15) sts, 2 sc in next st, sc in next 4 (5, 6) sts] 3 times—57 (63, 69) sts.

Rnd 12 (13, 14): [Sc in next 1 (2, 3) st(s), 2 sc in next st, sc in next 17 (18, 19) sts] 3 times—60 (66, 72) sts.

Rnds 13-22 (14-24, 15-26): Sc in each st around.

Rnd 23 (25, 27): Sc in next 42 (46, 50) sts, leaving rest of rnd unworked—42 (46, 50) sts. Do not fasten off. Work in turned rows to make earflaps as follows:

First Earflap

Row(s) 1 (1-3, 1-3): (WS) Ch 1, turn, sc in next 42 (46, 50) sts—42 (46, 50) sts.

Row 2 (4, 4): Ch 1, turn, sc2tog, sc in next 40 (44, 48) sts—41 (45, 49) sts.

Row 3 (5, 5): Ch 1, turn, sc2tog, sc in next 39 (43, 47) sts—40 (44, 48) sts.

Row 4 (6, 6): Ch 1, turn, sc2tog, sc in next 13 (14, 15) sts, leaving remainder of sts in row unworked—14 (15, 16) sts.

Row 5 (7, 7): Ch 1, turn, sc2tog, sc in next 12 (13, 14) sts—13 (14, 15) sts.

Row 6 (8, 8): Ch 1, turn, sc2og, sc in next 11 (12, 13) sts—12 (13, 14) sts.

Row 7 (9, 9): Ch 1, turn, sc2tog, sc in next 10 (11, 12) sts—11 (12, 13) sts.

Row 8 (10, 10): Ch 1, turn, sc2tog, sc in next 9 (10, 11) sts—10 (11, 12) sts.

Row 9 (11, 11): Ch 1, turn, sc2tog, sc in next 8 (9, 10) sts—9 (10, 11) sts.

Row 10 (12, 12): Ch 1, turn, sc2tog, sc in next 7 (8, 9) sts—8 (9, 10) sts.

Row 11 (13, 13): Ch 1, turn, sc2tog, sc in next 6 (7, 8) sts—7 (8, 9) sts.

Sizes Medium and Large only
Row 14: Ch 1, turn, sc2tog, sc in next 6 (7) sts—7 (8) sts.

Size Large only
Row 15: Ch 1, turn, sc2tog, sc in next 6 sts—7 sts.

All Sizes
Next row: Ch 1, turn, sc2tog, sc in next 3 sts, sc2tog—5 sts.

Next row: Ch 1, turn, sc2tog, sc in next st, sc2tog—3 sts.

Next row: Ch 1, turn, sc3tog—1 st. Do not fasten off.

Edging
Ch 1, with RS facing, sc 9 (11, 12) down back edge of earflap, sc in next 25 (28, 31) sts across back neck to other side of hat. Do not fasten off.

Second Earflap
Next row: Ch 1, turn, sc2tog, sc in next 12 (13, 14) sts—13 (14, 15) sts.

Follow instructions for first earflap starting with Row 6 (8, 8). Do not fasten off.

Edging
Ch 1, with RS facing, sc 14 (15, 16) down the front edge of the earflap. Working across front of hat, sc in next 18 (20, 22) sts, sc 14 (15, 16) up front of other earflap, sl st to fasten off. With RS facing and hat upside down, join yarn at back edge of remaining unbound earflap edge. Work 9 (11, 12) sc along back edge of earflap, sl st to fasten off.

Ears
Rnd 1: With CC1 make an adjustable ring, 6 sc in ring. Pull on beg tail to tighten ring—6 sts. Pm to keep track of beg of rnds.

Rnd 2: 2 sc in each st around—12 sts.

Rnd 3: [2 sc in next st, sc in next 3 sts] 3 times—15 sts.

Rnd 4: [Sc in next 2 sts, 2 sc in next st, sc in next 2 sts] 3 times—18 sts.

Sizes Medium and Large only
Rnd 5: [Sc in next 5 sts, 2 sc in next st] 3 times—21 sts.

All Sizes
Rnds 5-7 (6-8, 6-9): Sc in each st around.

Rnd 8 (9, 10): [Sc in next 4 (5, 5) sts, sc2tog] 3 times—15 (18, 18) sts.

Fasten off, leaving long tail for sewing.

Face
With CC1, ch 12 (13, 15).

Rnd 1: Working in bottom ridge lp of ch (see Stitch Guide), 2 sc in 2nd ch from hook (the first ch from hook does not count as st), sc in next 9 (10, 12) ch, 2 sc in next ch, rotate work 180 degrees, like you're turning a steering wheel, keep the same side facing, to work across the opposite edge of the fnd ch as foll: 2 sc in next st, sc in next 9 (10, 12) sts, 2 sc in next st—26 (28, 32) sts around. Do not join, but continue to work in a spiral. Pm to keep track of beg of rnds.

Rnd 2: [2 sc in next 2 sts, sc in next 9 (10, 12) sts, 2 sc in next 2 sts] twice—34 (36, 40) sts. Work 1 sc to shift beg of rnd. First st of next rnd will count as beg of rnd.

Sizes Medium and Large only
Rnd 3: [Sc in next st, 2 sc in next st, sc in next 14 (16) sts, 2 sc in next st, sc in next st] twice—40 (44) sts.

All Sizes
Rnd 3 (4, 4): Sc in next st, 2 sc in next st, sc in next 0 (1, 1) st(s), sk next st, 7 dc in next st, sk next st, sc in next 7 (8, 10) sts, sk next st, 7 dc in next st, sk next st, sc in next 0 (1, 1) st(s), 2 sc in next st, sc in next 1 (2, 2) st(s), 2 sc in next 2 sts, sc in next 13 (14, 16) sts, 2 sc in next 2 sts, sc in next 0 (1, 1) st(s)—48 (54, 58) sts.

Sizes Small and Large only
Rnd 4 (5): Sc in next 3 (4) sts, [hdc in next st, 2 hdc in next st] 3 times, hdc in next st, sk next st, sc in next 5 (8) sts, sk next st [hdc in next st, 2 hdc in next st] 3 times, hdc in next st, sc in next 5 (7) sts, 2 sc in next st, sc in next 15 (18) sts, 2 sc in next 2 (3) sts, sl st to fasten off, leaving long tail for sewing—54 (64) sts.

Size Medium only
Rnd 5: Sc in next 4 sts, [hdc in next st, 2 hdc in next st] 3 times, hdc in next st, sk next st, sc in next 6 sts, sk next st [hdc in next st, 2 hdc in next st] 3 times, hdc in next st, sc in next 4 sts, leave remaining sts of rnd unworked,

sl st to fasten off, leaving long tail for sewing—34 sts worked in this round, 58 sts around (total), 4 increases made.

Snout

Rnd 1: With CC1 make an adjustable ring, 6 sc in ring. Pull on beg tail to tighten ring—6 sts. Pm to keep track of beg of rnds.

Rnd 2: [2 sc in next st, sc in next st] 3 times—9 sts.

Rnd 3: [2 sc in next st, sc in next 2 sts] 3 times—12 sts.

Rnd 4: [2 sc in next st, sc in next 3 sts] 3 times—15 sts.

Rnd 5: [2 sc in next st, sc in next 4 sts] 3 times—18 sts.

Rnd 6: [2 sc in next st, sc in next 5 sts] 3 times—21 sts.

Size Small only

Fasten off, leaving a long tail for sewing.

Sizes Medium and Large only

Rnd 7: [2 sc in next st, sc in next 6 sts] 3 times—24 sts.

Size Medium only

Fasten off, leaving a long tail for sewing.

Size Large only

Rnd 8: [2 sc in next st, sc in next 7 sts] 3 times—27 sts.

Fasten off, leaving a long tail for sewing.

Coat Base

Rnd 1: With CC2 make an adjustable ring, 6 sc in ring. Pull on beg tail to tighten ring—6 sts. Pm to keep track of beg of rnds.

Rnd 2: 2 sc blo around—12 sts. Place contrasting st marker in the first unused lp of rnd. Leave in place until you begin to add the hairs to coat.

Rnd 3: [2 sc blo in next st, sc blo in next st] 6 times—18 sts.

Rnd 4: [Sc blo in next st, 2 sc blo in next st, sc blo in next st] 6 times—24 sts.

Rnd 5: [Sc blo in next 3 sts, 2 sc blo in next st] 6 times—30 sts.

Sizes Medium and Large only

Rnd 6: [2 sc blo in next st, sc blo in next 4 sts] 6 times—36 sts.

Size Large only

Rnd 7: [Sc blo in next 2 sts, 2 sc blo in next st, sc blo in next 3 sts] 6 times—42 sts.

All Sizes

Rnd 6 (7, 8): [Sc blo in next 3 (3, 4) sts, 2 sc blo in next st] 3 times, sc blo in next 1 (4, 4) st(s). Leave remaining sts unworked—16 (19, 22) sts. Do not fasten off.

CONTINUE COAT

Note: You will be working in turned rows.

Row 1 and all WS rows: (WS) Ch 1, turn, sc flo across.

Row 2: (RS) Ch 1, turn, [2 sc blo in next st, sc blo in next 4 (5, 6) sts] 3 times, 2 sc blo in last st—20 (23, 26 sts).

Row 4: Ch 1, turn, [2 sc blo in next st, sc blo in next 5 (6, 7) sts] 3 times, sc blo in next st, 2 sc blo in next st—24 (27, 30) sts.

Rows 6 and 8: Ch 1, turn, sc blo across.

Row 10: Ch 1, turn, sc2tog in blo, sc blo in next 20 (23, 26) sts, sc2tog in blo—22 (25, 28) sts.

Row 11: Ch 1, turn, sc flo across.

Sizes Medium and Large only
Row 12: Ch 1, turn, sc blo across—25 (28) sts.

Row 13: Ch 1, turn, sc flo across.

All Sizes
Row 12 (14, 14): Ch 1, turn, sc2tog in blo, sc blo in next 18 (21, 24) sts, sc2tog in blo—20 (23, 26) sts.

Row 13 (15, 15): Ch 1, turn, sc flo across.

Size Large only
Row 16: Ch 1, turn, sc blo across—26 sts.

Row 17: Ch 1, turn, sc flo across.

All Sizes
Row 14 (16, 18): Ch 1, turn, sc2tog in blo, sc blo in next 16 (19, 22) sts, sc2tog in blo—18 (21, 24) sts.

Row 15 (17, 19): Ch 1, turn, sc flo across.

Row 16 (18, 20): Ch 1, turn, sc2tog in blo 1 (2, 2) time(s), sc blo in next 14 (13, 16) sts, sc2tog in blo 1 (2, 2) time(s)—16 (17, 20) sts.

Row 17 (19, 21): Ch 1, turn, sc flo across. Fasten off, leaving long tail for sewing.

Coat Edging

With RS facing, join new yarn of CC2 to indented corner of coat. If left-handed, bottom edge of coat is at left; if right-handed, bottom edge of coat is at right. Work 15 (16, 18) sc along side edges of turned rows ending at bottom edge of coat. Working into sts at bottom edge of coat: sc2tog twice, sc in next 8 (9, 12) sts, sc2tog twice—12 (13, 16) sts. Rotate coat and work 15 (16, 18) sc up opposite side of row-ends ending at other indented corner. Fasten off, leaving long tail for sewing.

Adding Hairs to Coat

Note: When adding hairs to coat, keep in mind that there will be many hairs close tog, so it is okay if you miss a hair, or add an extra hair, or sl st here or there; it won't show. You may want to add an extra st, or leave one out, to adjust placement of hairs as you go. This looks best if hairs do not line up perfectly in vertical columns; they should be staggered. Follow basic formula of working about 3 sl sts in unused lps in coat between hairs. At end of a row, make a ch before rotating to work back along next row of unused lps. Ch counts as a sl st. See notes for definition of hair stitch (Hs).

Keeping RS facing now and throughout, pull up CC2 from first unused lp at center top of coat (marked with contrast marker), *sl st in next unused lp, Hs (see Stitch Guide), sl st in next 2 unused lps**; rep from * to ** around entire section of coat base that was worked in the rnd. At section that was worked in turned rows, work from * to ** across each row. At end of a row, ch 1 (counts as sl st), keeping RS facing, rotate work 180 degrees to work along next row of unused lps. Cont to work in this st patt, back and forth across all unused lps along coat. Fasten off, leaving long tail for sewing.

Finishing

Block all pieces if desired. Use yarn tails and yarn needle to stitch all pieces to hat as follows: Pin and stitch face to front of hat. Bottom of face should line up with front bottom edge of hat. Pin, then stitch coat and ears to hat using photo as a guide. Center section of coat that was worked in the rnd should be placed slightly forward from center top of hat. Line up bottom edge of coat with bottom edge of back of hat. Ears should be placed just in front of indented corners of coat. Bottom edge of ears should be curled into a shallow C shape. This helps ears stand up on their own. Stuff snout lightly with polyester stuffing and pin to face using photos as a placement guide. Using yarn tails and yarn needle, stitch muzzle to face. With black embroidery floss and embroidery needle, use satin stitch (see Glossary) to embroider a triangle on tip of snout for nose. Embroider a vertical line that extends downward from bottom tip of triangle, and a V shape at bottom end of this line for a mouth.

TIE ENDS
Cut 12 pieces of MC each 36" (91.5 cm) long. Group 6 pieces tog for each tie and find center by folding them in half. Insert hook through bottom point of earflap and place center of group of yarn on hook. Using your hook, pull center of all 6 strands (held tog) through tip of earflap. Make this lp big enough to reach through it with fingers or a hook and pull all cut ends through. Carefully pull on yarn to tighten lp. Rep process for other earflap. Separate out strands into 3 groups, with 4 strands in each group. Braid each tie until braid measures about 6" (15 cm). Tie end in knot and trim ends neatly.

Sophie
RAGLAN PULLOVER

DESIGNED BY KATYA NOVIKOVA

This simple sweater is baby's new wardrobe staple. The silhouette is classic, and the possible color combinations are endless. The hand-dyed yarn makes a beautiful finished fabric, and the sweater would be the envy of any shower. Not to worry, though! It's machine washable.

FINISHED SIZE
Instructions are written for size 3–6 months. Changes for 6–12 months, 12–18 months, 18–24 months, and 2–3 years are in parentheses.

Chest circumference: 18 (19, 21, 21½, 24½)" (45.5 [48.5, 53.5, 54.5, 62] cm).

Shown in size 18–24 months.

YARN
Sportweight (#2 Fine).

Shown here: Madelinetosh Tosh Sport (100% superwash merino; 270 yd [247 m]/3½ oz [100 g]): antler (MC), 1 (1, 2, 2, 2) skein(s); winter wheat (CC), 1 skein.

HOOK
Size D/3 (3.25 mm). *Adjust hook size if necessary to obtain correct gauge.*

NOTIONS
Stitch markers; yarn needle.

GAUGE
17 sts and 18 rows = 4" (10 cm) in patt st. (See instructions for gauge swatch below.)

NOTES
Sleeves, back, and front are worked separately from the top down.

Ribbing edging is worked after pieces are sewn together.

GAUGE SWATCH

Ch 18.

Row 1: (WS) Sc in 2nd ch from hook, *dc in next ch, sc in next ch; rep from * to end—17 sts.

Row 2: (RS) Ch 1, sc in first st and in each st across.

Row 3: Ch 3 (counts as dc), *sc in next st, dc in next st; rep from * to end.

Row 4: Rep Row 2.

Row 5: Ch 1, sc in first st, *dc in next st, sc in next st; rep from * to end.

Rows 6-13: Rep Rows 2-5 two more times.

Rows 14-16: Rep Rows 2-4. Fasten off.

Sleeve (make 2)

With CC, ch 11 (11, 13, 13, 15).

Row 1: (WS) (inc) (Sc, dc) in 2nd ch from hook, *sc in next ch, dc in next ch; rep from * to last st, (sc, dc) in last st—12 (12, 14, 14, 16) sts.

Row 2: (RS) Ch 1, sc in each st across.

Row 3: (inc) Ch 1, (sc, dc) in first st, *sc in next st, dc in next st; rep from * to last st, [dc, sc] in last st—14 (14, 16, 16, 18) sts.

Rep Rows 2 and 3 six (six, seven, seven, eight) times—26 (26, 30, 30, 34) sts.

Row 16 (16, 18, 18, 20): Ch 1, 2 sc in first st, sc in each st across, ending with 2 sc in last st—28 (28, 32, 32, 36) sts. Place markers (pm) in first and last sc.

Sizes 3-6 (12-18) Months only
Row 17 (19): Ch 1, sc in first st, *dc in next st, sc in next st; rep from * to last st, dc in last st—28 (32) sts.

Row 18 (20): Ch 1, sc in each st across.

Row 19 (21): Ch 3 (counts as dc), *sc in next st, dc in next st; rep from * to last st, sc in last st.

Row 20 (22): Ch 1, sc in each st across.

Row 21 (23): Ch 1, sc in first st, *dc in next st, sc in next st; rep from * to last st, dc in last st.

Rep Rows 18-21 (20-23) six times.

Size 12-18 Months only
Rep Rows 20 and 21 once more.

Fasten off all sizes.

Sizes 6-12 Months (18-24 Months, 2-3 Years) only
Row 17 (19, 21): (Ch 3 [counts as dc], sc) in first st, *dc in next st, sc in next st; rep from * to last st, (dc, sc) in last st—30 (34, 38) sts.

Row 18 (20, 22): Ch 1, sc in each st across.

Row 19 (21, 23): Ch 1, sc in first st, *dc in next st, sc in next st; rep from * to last st, dc in last st.

Row 20 (22, 24): Ch 1, sc in each st across.

Row 21 (23, 25): Ch 3 (counts as dc), *sc in next st, dc in next st; rep from * to last st, sc in last st.

Rep Rows 18-21 (20-23, 22-25) six (six, seven) times.

Sizes 6-12 Months (2-3 Years) only
Rep Rows 18 and 19 (22 and 23) once more.

Fasten off all sizes.

Back and Front (make 2)

With MC, ch 21 (21, 25, 25, 29).

Row 1: (WS) (inc) [Sc, dc] in 2nd ch from hook, *sc in next st, dc in next st; rep from * to last st, (sc, dc) in last st—22 (22, 26, 26, 30) sts.

Row 2: (RS) Ch 1, sc in first and each st across.

Row 3: (inc) Ch 1, (sc, dc) in first st, *sc in next st, dc in next st; rep from * to last st, (sc, dc) in last st—24 (24, 28, 28, 32) sts.

Rep Rows 2 and 3 six (six, seven, seven, eight) times—36 (36, 42, 42, 48) sts.

Row 16 (16, 18, 18, 20): (inc) Ch 1, 2 sc in first st, sc in each st across to last st, 2 sc in last st—38 (38, 44, 44, 50) sts. Pm in first and last sc.

Sizes 3-6 (12-18) Months only
Row 17 (19): Ch 1, sc in first st, *dc in next st, sc in next st; rep from * to last st, dc in last st—38 (44) sts.

Row 18 (20): Ch 1, sc in first and each st across.

Row 19 (21): Ch 3 (counts as dc), *sc in next st, dc in next st; rep from * to last st, sc in last st.

Row 20 (22): Ch 1, sc in first and each st across.

Row 21 (23): Ch 1, sc in first st, *dc in next st, sc in next st; rep from * to last st, dc in last st.

Sizes 6-12 Months (18-24 Months, 2-3 Years) only
Row 17 (19, 21): (inc) (Ch 3 [counts as dc], sc) in first st, *dc in next st, sc in next st; rep from * to last st, (dc, sc) in next st—40 (46, 52) sts.

Row 18 (20, 22): Ch 1, sc in first and each st across.

Row 19 (21, 23): Ch 1, sc in first st, *dc in next st, sc in next st; rep from * to last st, dc in last st.

Row 20 (22, 24): Ch 1, sc in first and each st across.

Row 21 (23, 25): Ch 3 (counts as dc), *sc in next st, dc in next st; rep from * to last st, sc in last st.

All Sizes
Rep Rows 18-21 (18-21, 20-23, 20-23, 22-25) six (six, six, seven, seven) times.

Sizes 6-12 (12-18) Months only
Rep Rows 18 and 19 (20 and 21) once more.

Fasten off all sizes.

Finishing

Sew front and back side seams together from bottom edge to marker. Sew sleeve seams from wrist edge to

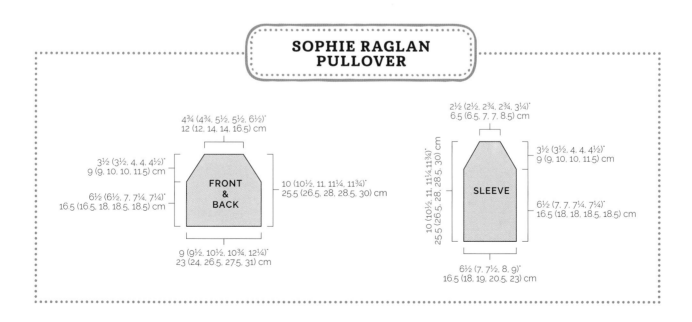

SOPHIE RAGLAN PULLOVER

4¾ (4¾, 5½, 5½, 6½)"
12 (12, 14, 14, 16.5) cm

3½ (3½, 4, 4, 4½)"
9 (9, 10, 10, 11.5) cm

FRONT & BACK

10 (10½, 11, 11¼, 11¾)"
25.5 (26.5, 28, 28.5, 30) cm

6½ (6½, 7, 7¼, 7¼)"
16.5 (16.5, 18, 18.5, 18.5) cm

9 (9½, 10½, 10¾, 12¼)"
23 (24, 26.5, 27.5, 31) cm

2½ (2½, 2¾, 2¾, 3¼)"
6.5 (6.5, 7, 7, 8.5) cm

3½ (3½, 4, 4, 4½)"
9 (9, 10, 10, 11.5) cm

SLEEVE

10 (10½, 11, 11¼, 11¾)"
25.5 (26.5, 28, 28.5, 30) cm

6½ (7, 7, 7¼, 7¼)"
16.5 (18, 18, 18.5, 18.5) cm

6½ (7, 7½, 8, 9)"
16.5 (18, 19, 20.5, 23) cm

marker. Remove markers. Sew raglan sleeve edges to raglan bodice edges.

SLEEVE EDGING

Join CC to any st of last row of sleeve on inner side, near seam.

Rnd 1: Ch 1, work 28 (30, 32, 34, 38) sc evenly around, join with sl st in first st, do not turn.

Size 3–6 Months only

Rnds 2–5: Ch 1, [sc flo in next 3 sts, sc blo in next 2 sts] 5 times, sc flo in next 2 sts, sc blo in last st, join with sl st in first sc, do not turn—28 sts. Fasten off.

Size 6–12 Months only

Rnds 2–5: Ch 1, [sc flo in next 3 sts, sc blo in next 2 sts] 6 times, join with sl st in first sc, do not turn—30 sts. Fasten off.

Size 12–18 Months only

Rnds 2–5: Ch 1, [sc flo in next 3 sts, sc blo in next 2 sts] 5 times, sc flo in next 4 sts, sc blo in next 3 sts, join with sl st in first sc, do not turn—32 sts. Fasten off.

Size 18–24 Months only

Rnds 2–5: Ch 1, [sc flo in next 3 sts, sc blo in next 2 sts] 6 times, sc flo in next 3 sts, sc blo in last st, join with sl st in first sc, do not turn—34 sts. Fasten off.

Size 2–3 Years only

Rnds 2–5: Ch 1, [sc flo in next 3 sts, sc blo in next 2 sts] 7 times, sc flo in next 2 sts, sc blo in last st, join with sl st in first sc, do not turn—38 sts. Fasten off.

Rep for second sleeve.

NECK EDGING

Join CC to any st of back foundation ch near seam.

Rnd 1: Ch 1, 60 (60, 72, 72, 84) sc evenly around, join with sl st in first sc, do not turn.

Sizes 3–6 (6–12) Months only
Rnds 2–4: Ch 1, [sc flo in next 3 sts, sc blo in next 2 sts] 12 times, join with sl st in first sc, do not turn—60 sts. Fasten off.

Sizes 12–18 (18–24) Months only
Rnds 2–4: Ch 1, [sc flo in next 3 sts, sc blo in next 2 sts] 13 times, sc flo in next 4 sts, sc blo in next 3 sts, join with sl st in first sc, do not turn—72 sts. Fasten off.

Size 2–3 Years only
Rnds 2–4: Ch 1, [sc flo in next 3 sts, sc blo in next 2 sts] 16 times, sc flo in next 3 sts, sc blo in last st, join with sl st in beg sc, do not turn—84 sts. Fasten off.

BOTTOM EDGING
Join CC to any st of last row of back, near seam.

Rnd 1: Ch 1, 76 (80, 88, 92, 104) sc evenly around, join with sl st in first sc, do not turn.

Size 3–6 Months only
Rnds 2–4: Ch 1, [sc flo in next 3 sts, sc blo in next 2 sts] 15 times, sc blo in last st, join with sl st in first sc, do not turn—76 sts. Fasten off.

Size 6–12 Months only
Rnds 2–4: Ch 1, [sc flo in next 3 sts, sc blo in next 2 sts] 16 times, join with sl st in first sc, do not turn—80 sts. Fasten off.

Size 12–18 Months only
Rnds 2–4: Ch 1, [sc flo in next 3 sts, sc blo in next 2 sts] 15 times, sc flo in next 3 sts, sc blo in next 3 sts, sc flo in next 4 sts, sc blo in next 3 sts, join with sl st

in first sc, do not turn—88 sts, fasten off.

Size 18–24 Months only
Rnds 2–4: Ch 1, [sc flo in next 3 sts, sc blo in next 2 sts] 16 times, [sc flo in next 3 sts, sc blo in next 3 sts] twice, join with sl st in first sc, do not turn—92 sts. Fasten off.

Size 2–3 Years only
Rnds 2–4: Ch 1, [sc flo in next 3 sts, sc blo in next 2 sts] 20 times, sc flo in next 3 sts, sc blo in last st, join with

sl st in first sc, do not turn—100 sts. Fasten off.

Finishing
Weave in ends. Block to measurements.

Landon

FAUX CABLED PULLOVER

DESIGNED BY ROBYN CHACHULA

Cabled sweaters look so adorable on babies, but they can be too stiff and bulky for active wee ones. This sweater uses slip-stitch embroidery to make faux cables. The weight of the fabric is perfect to keep little ones warm, yet light enough for them to move about.

FINISHED SIZE
Instructions are written for size Newborn–6 months. Changes for 6–12 months, 12–18 months, and 18–24 months are in parentheses.

Chest circumference: 21 (22½, 24½, 26½)" (53.5 [57, 62, 67.5] cm). Shown in size 12–18 months.

YARN
Sportweight (#2 Fine).

Shown here: Neighborhood Fiber Co. Studio DK (100% superwash merino; 275 yd [251 m]/4 oz [113 g]): Thomas Circle, 2 (2, 3, 3) hanks.

HOOK
Size 7 (4.5 mm). *Adjust hook size if necessary to obtain correct gauge.*

NOTIONS
Yarn needle; two ½" (13 mm) buttons; matching sewing thread.

GAUGE
17 sc and 16 rows = 4" (10 cm).

NOTES
Sizes Newborn–6 months and 6–12 months have a 6-row rep (Rows 6–11) for cable; 12–18 months and 18–24 months have an 8-row rep (Rows 6–13) for more elongated cables.

Faux cables are created using slip-stitch embroidery after completion of the front and back panels (see Faux Cable charts).

Front Panel

Ch 45, 49, 53, 57.

Row 1: Sc in 2nd ch from hook, sc in next 3 (5, 3, 5) ch, *ch 1, sk next ch, sc in next 2 ch, ch 1, sk next ch**, sc in next 4 ch; rep from * across to last 4 (6, 4, 6) ch ending at **, sc in each ch across to end—44, 48, 52, 56 sts.

Row 2: Ch 1, *sc in each sc to ch-sp, ch 1, sk ch-sp; rep from * across to last 4 (6, 4, 6) sc, sc in each sc to end.

Rows 3–5: Rep Row 2.

Row 6: Ch 1, sc in next 4 (6, 4, 6) sc, *sc in next ch-sp, ch 2, sk 2 sc, sc in next ch-sp, sc in next 4 sc; rep from * across to last 4 (6, 4, 6) sc, sc in each sc across to end.

Row 7: Ch 1, *sc in each sc to ch-sp, ch 2, sk ch-sp; rep from * across to last 4 (6, 4, 6) sc, sc in each sc.

Row 8: Ch 1, sc in next 4 (6, 4, 6) sc, *ch 1, sk next sc, 2 sc in ch-2 sp, ch 1, sk next sc, sc in next 4 sc (st patt made); rep from * across, sc in each sc to end.

Row 9: Ch 1, * sc in each sc to ch-sp, ch 1, sk ch-sp; rep from * across, sc in each sc to end.

Rows 10 and 11 (10 and 11, 10–13, 10–13): Rep Row 9.

Rep patt Rows 6–11 (6–11, 6–13, 6–13) once more. Rep Rows 6–9 (6–9, 6–11, 6–11).

ARMHOLE SHAPING

Note: Cont to work in patt Rows 6–11 for sizes Newborn–6 months and 6–12 months, and Rows 6–13 for 12–18 months and 18–24 months, working shapings as follows:

Row 1: Sl st in first 0 (2, 3, 5) sc, sc2tog (see Glossary) over next 2 sts, work patt Row 10 (10, 12, 12) to last 2 (4, 5, 7) sts, sc2tog over next 2 sts, turn, leaving remaining sc unworked—42, (42, 44, 44) sts.

Row 2: Ch 1, sc2tog over first 2 sts, work patt Row 11 (11, 13, 13) across to last 2 sts, sc2tog over last 2 sts, turn—40 (40, 42, 42) sts.

Sizes Newborn–6 Months (6–12 Months) only

Row 3: Ch 1, sc2tog over first 2 sts, work patt Row 6 across to last 2 sc, sc2tog over last 2 sc—38 (38) sts.

Row 4: Ch 1, work patt Row 7 across to end.

Sizes 12–18 (18–24) Months only

Row 3: Ch 1, sc2tog over first 2 sts, work patt Row 6 to last 2 sts, sc2tog over last 2 sts—40 (40) sts.

Row 4: Ch 1, work patt Row 7 across to end.

Row 5: Ch 1, work patt Row 8 across to end.

Row 6: Ch 1, work patt Row 9 across to end.

Row 7: Ch 1, work patt Row 10 across to end.

Row 8: Ch 1, work patt Row 11 across to end.

NECK SHAPING
Sizes Newborn–6 Months (6–12 Months) only
First Side
Row 1: Ch 1, work patt Row 8 over first 8 sts, sc2tog over next 2 sts, turn, leaving remaining sts unworked—9 (9) sts.

Row 2: Ch 1, sc2tog over first 2 sc, work patt Row 9 across to end—8 (8) sts.

Row 3: Ch 1, work patt Row 10 to last 2 sts, sc2tog over last 2 sts, turn—7 (7) sts.

Row 4: Ch 1, work patt Row 11 across to end.

Row 5: Ch 1, work patt Row 6 across to end.

Row 6: Ch 1, work patt Row 7 across to end.

Rows 7–10: Ch 1, work patt Rows 8–11 across to end. Fasten off.

Second Side
Row 1: Sk 18 sts from end of Row 1 (first side of neck shaping), join yarn with sl st in next st, sc in next sc, work patt Row 8 across to end—9 (9) sts.

Row 2: Ch 1, work patt Row 9 to last 2 sc, sc2tog over next 2 sts—8 (8) sts.

Row 3: Ch 1, sc2tog first 2 sts, work patt Row 10 across to end—7 (7) sts.

Row 4: Ch 1, work patt Row 11 across to end.

Row 5: Ch 1, work patt Row 6 across to end.

Row 6: Ch 1, work patt Row 7 across to end.

Rows 7–10: Ch 1, work patt Rows 8–11 across to end. Fasten off.

Sizes 12–18 (18–24) Months only
First Side
Row 1: Ch 1, work patt Row 12 over first 7 sts, sc2tog over next 2 sc, turn, leaving remaining sts unworked—8 (8) sts.

Row 2: Ch 1, sc2tog over first 2 sts, work patt Row 13 to end—7 (7) sts.

Row 3: Ch 1, work patt Row 6 to last 2 sts, sc2tog over last 2 sc—6 (6) sts.

Row 4: Ch 1, work patt Row 7 across to end.

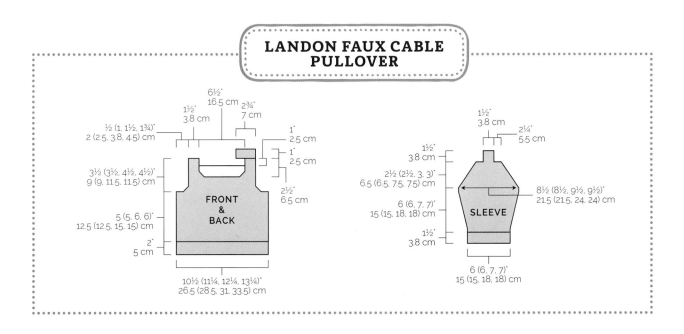

LANDON FAUX CABLE PULLOVER

6½"
16.5 cm

2¾"
7 cm

1½"
3.8 cm

½ (1, 1½, 1¾)"
2 (2.5, 3.8, 4.5) cm

1"
2.5 cm

1"
2.5 cm

3½ (3½, 4½, 4½)"
9 (9, 11.5, 11.5) cm

2½"
6.5 cm

FRONT & BACK

5 (5, 6, 6)"
12.5 (12.5, 15, 15) cm

2"
5 cm

10½ (11¼, 12¼, 13¼)"
26.5 (28.5, 31, 33.5) cm

1½"
3.8 cm

2¼"
5.5 cm

1½"
3.8 cm

2½ (2½, 3, 3)"
6.5 (6.5, 7.5, 7.5) cm

6 (6, 7, 7)"
15 (15, 18, 18) cm

SLEEVE

8½ (8½, 9½, 9½)"
21.5 (21.5, 24, 24) cm

1½"
3.8 cm

6 (6, 7, 7)"
15 (15, 18, 18) cm

FAUX CABLE PATTERN

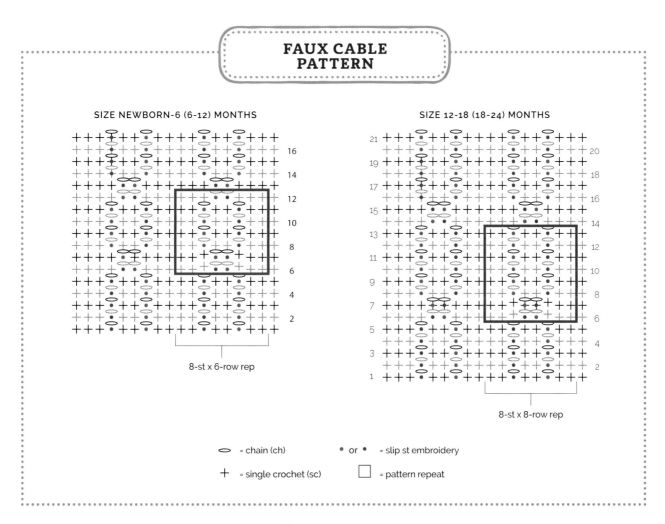

SIZE NEWBORN-6 (6-12) MONTHS

8-st x 6-row rep

SIZE 12-18 (18-24) MONTHS

8-st x 8-row rep

⬭ = chain (ch)

● or ● = slip st embroidery

+ = single crochet (sc)

□ = pattern repeat

Rows 5–10: Ch 1, work patt Rows 8–13 across to end. Fasten off.

Second Side

Row 1: Sk 22 sts from end of Row 1 (first side of neck shaping), join with sl st in next sc, sc in next sc, work patt Row 12 across to end—8 (8) sts.

Row 2: Ch 1, work patt Row 13 over first 6 sts, sc2tog over last 2 sts—7 (7) sts.

Row 3: Ch 1, sc2tog over first 2 sts, work patt Row 6 to end—6 (6) sts.

Row 4: Ch 1, work patt Row 7 across to end.

Rows 5–10: Ch 1, work patt Rows 8–13 across to end. Fasten off.

Back Panel

Rep instructions for front panel through Row 4 (4, 8, 8) of armhole shaping.

Sizes Newborn–6 Months (6–12 Months) only

Row 5: Ch 1, sc in first sc, work patt Row 8 across to end—38 (38) sts.

Rows 6–8: Ch 1, work patt Rows 9–11 across to end.

Row 9: Ch 1, work patt Row 6 across to end.

Row 10: Ch 1, work patt Row 7 across to end.

NECK SHAPING

First Side

Row 11: Ch 1, work patt Row 8 over first 7 sts, turn, leaving remaining sts unworked—7 (7) sts.

Rows 12–14: Ch 1, work patt Rows 9–11 across to end. Fasten off.

Second Side

Row 11: Sk 23 sts from end of Row 11 (first side of neck shaping), join with sl st in next sc, ch 1, work patt Row 8 across to end—7 (7) sts.

Rows 12–14: Ch 1, work patt Rows 9–11 across to end. Fasten off.

Sizes 12–18 (18–24) Months only

Rows 9 and 10: Ch 1, work patt Rows 12 and 13 across to end.

Rows 11 and 12: Ch 1, work patt Rows 6 and 7 across to end.

Rows 13 and 14: Ch 1, work patt Rows 8 and 9 across to end.

NECK SHAPING
First Side
Row 15: Ch 1, work patt Row 10 over first 6 sts, turn, leaving remaining sts unworked—6 (6) sts.

Rows 16–18: Ch 1, work patt Rows 11–13 across to end. Fasten off.

Second Side
Row 15: Sk 27 sts from end of Row 15 (first side of neck shaping), join with sl st in next sc, ch 1, work patt Row 10 across to end—6 (6) sts.

Rows 16–18: Ch 1, work patt Rows 11–13 across to end. Fasten off.

Sleeve (make 2)
Ch 27 (27, 31, 31).

Row 1: Sc in 2nd ch from hook, sc in each ch across, turn—26 (26, 30, 30) sc.

Sizes 12–18 (18–24) Months only
Rows 2 and 3: Ch 1, sc in each sc across, turn.

All Sizes
Row 2 (2, 4, 4): Ch 1, 2 sc in first sc, sc in each sc across to last sc, 2 sc in last sc, turn—28 (28, 32, 32) sc.

Rows 3–6 (3–6, 5–8, 5–8): Ch 1, sc in each sc across.

Rep last 5 rows 3 more times—34 (34, 38, 38) sts.

Row 22 (22, 24, 24): Rep Row 2 (2, 4, 4)—36 (36, 40, 40) sts.

Rows 23 and 24 (23 and 24, 25 and 26, 25 and 26): Ch 1, sc in each sc across.

CAP SHAPING

Row 1: Ch 1, sc2tog over first 2 sc, sc in each sc to last 2 sc, sc2tog over last 2 sc, turn—34 (34, 38, 38) sts.

Rep Row 1 nine (nine, eleven, eleven) more times—16 (16, 16, 16) sts.

SHOULDER SADDLE

Row 1: Sl st in next 5 sc, ch 1, sc in next 6 sc, turn, leaving remaining sts unworked—6 sc.

Rows 2–6: Ch 1, sc in each sc across. Fasten off.

Finishing

Pin panels to schematic size, spray with water, and allow to dry.

Slip-stitch embroider (see Glossary) on ch-1 sps to create faux cables by joining yarn to bottom edge at any ch-sp. Using chart as a guide, sl st around next ch-1 sp by inserting hook from RS to WS and pulling up a lp from back to sl st over ch-sp. Rep up along panel to top for both sides of cable and crossing left ch over right ch at the ch-2 sps to create right cables. Fasten off. Weave in ends.

Place RS of back and front panel tog. Whipstitch (see Glossary) side seams and turn RS out. Set in sleeve with RS facing. Whipstitch around sleeve and shoulder saddle. Whipstitch underarm seam. Rep on other sleeve, but only seam one side of shoulder saddle. Leave other open for collar edging.

BOTTOM RIBBING

Join yarn to bottom edge of back with sl st, ch 9.

Row 1: Sc in 2nd ch from hook, sc in each ch across, sl st twice to bottom edge (once to join and once to act as turning ch), turn—8 sts.

Row 2: Sk both sl st, sc blo in each sc across, turn.

Row 3: Ch 1, sc blo in each sc across, sl st twice to edge, turn.

Rep Rows 2 and 3 around edge to beg. Fasten off.

Whipstitch first and last rows tog. Weave in ends.

CUFFS

Join yarn to cuff edge at seam, ch 7.

Rep instructions as for bottom ribbing over 6 sts.

COLLAR

Join yarn to edge of collar on RS.

Row 1: Ch 1, sc evenly around neck opening to opposite side, turn.

Row 2: Ch 1, sc in each sc to outside corner, 3 sc in outside corner, *sc in each sc to inside corner, sc2tog over center 2 sc of inside corner; rep from * around, 3 sc in outside corner, sc in each sc to end, turn.

Row 3: Ch 1, sc in next 2 sc, ch 2, sk 2 sc, sc in next 3 sc, ch 2, sk 2 sc, cont with Rnd 2 instructions across.

Row 4: Cont in Rnd 2 instructions to ch-sps, 2 sc in each ch-sp, sc in each sc, turn.

Rnd 5: Rep Rnd 2. Fasten off.

Weave in ends.

Sew buttons to shoulder opposite buttonholes.

Ava
CLOTH DIAPER WRAP

DESIGNED BY ANASTASIA POPOVA

This adjustable diaper cover would make a welcome gift for any cloth-diapering mama-to-be. This "soaker" will fit well over flat or pre-folded diapers. You could also sew in a flannel pocket and use this wrap with inserts.

FINISHED SIZE

Instructions are written for size Newborn-6 months. Changes for 6-12 months, 12-18 months, and 18-24 months are in parentheses.

Rise: 7 (8, 9, 10)" (18 [20.5, 23, 25.5] cm).

Shown in size 18-24 months.

YARN

Worsted weight (#4 Medium).

Shown here: Patons Classic Wool Worsted (100% pure new wool; 210 yd [192 m]/3½ oz [100 g]): #77531 currant, 1 skein.

HOOK

Size G/6 (4 mm). *Adjust hook size if necessary to obtain correct gauge.*

NOTIONS

Four ½" (13 mm) buttons (for closure); two 1" (25 mm) flat buttons (for embellishment); yarn needle; matching thread and sewing needle (for buttons).

GAUGE

22 sts and 8 rows = 4" (10 cm) in hdc blo.

NOTES

The wrap is worked sideways in stitches of different height to create shaping.

Large buttons on the outside at back top edge are for decorative purposes. Four buttons on inside are for buttoning diaper cover in place.

There are two sets of buttonholes at front top edge. For two lower buttons, any space between hdc can be used as a buttonhole to achieve best fit.

Foundation half double crochet (Fhdc): Ch 2, yo, insert hook in 2nd ch from hook, yo and pull up lp (3 lps on hook), yo and draw through 1 lp (1 chain made), yo and draw through all lps on hook—*1 Fhdc made.* *Yo, insert hook under the 2 lps of the "chain" stitch of last stitch and pull up lp, yo and draw through 1 lp, yo and draw through all lps on hook; repeat from * for length of foundation.

Left Side

Row 1: (WS) Fhdc (see Stitch Guide) 62 (70, 80, 90), turn—62 (70, 80, 90) sts, turn.

Row 2: Ch 1 loosely (does not count as st throughout), hdc blo in each st across, turn.

Row 3: Ch 1, sc blo in next 10 (11, 12, 13) sts, hdc blo in next 22 (25, 29, 33) sts, sl st blo in next 12 (13, 14, 15) sts, hdc blo in next 8 (10, 13, 16) sts, sc blo in next 9 (10, 11, 12) sts, sc in last st, turn.

Row 4: Ch 1, sc blo in next 3 sts, (ch 1, sk next st)—*buttonhole made;* sc blo in next 6 (7, 8, 9) sts, hdc blo in next 8 (10, 13, 16) sts, sl st blo in next 12 (13, 14, 15) sts, hdc blo in next 22 (25, 29, 33) sts, sc blo in next 9 (10, 11, 12) sts, sc in last st, turn.

Rep Rows 3 and 4 once more.

Middle Section

Row 1: Ch 1, sc blo in next 10 (11, 12, 13) sts, hdc blo in next 22 (25, 29, 33) sts, sl st blo in next 12 (13, 14, 15) sts, hdc blo in next 8 (10, 13, 16) sts, sc blo in next 9 (10, 11, 12) sts, sc in last st, turn.

Row 2: Ch 1, sc blo in next 10 (11, 12, 13) sts, hdc blo in next 8 (10, 13, 16) sts, sl st blo in next 12 (13, 14, 15) sts, hdc blo in next 22 (25, 29, 33) sts, sc blo in next 9 (10, 11, 12) sts, sc in last st, turn.

Rep Rows 1 and 2 five (seven, eight, nine) more times.

Right Side

Row 1: Ch 1, sc blo in next 10 (11, 12, 13) sts, hdc blo in next 22 (25, 29, 33) sts, sl st blo in next 12 (13, 14, 15) sts, hdc blo in next 8 (10, 13, 16) sts, sc blo in next 6 (7, 8, 9) sts, (ch 1, sk next st)—*buttonhole made;* sc blo in next 2 sts, sc in last st, turn.

Row 2: Ch 1, sc blo in next 10 (11, 12, 13) sts, hdc blo in next 8 (10, 13, 16) sts, sl st blo in next 12 (13, 14, 15) sts, hdc blo in next 22 (25, 29, 33) sts, sc blo in next 9 (10, 11, 12) sts, sc in last st, turn.

Rep Rows 1 and 2 once more.

Rep Row 2 of left edge 2 times. Fasten off.

Finishing

Weave in ends. Attach 4 small buttons on the inside of the back half of the diaper wrap: 2 at each top corner and 2 about halfway along the edge. Attach 2 decorative buttons to the right side of the back half.

Charlie
BOOTIES

DESIGNED BY SHARON ZIENTARA

These booties were inspired by a DIY felt pair that I kept seeing all over the Internet. They work up quickly in a worsted-weight, washable wool so you can make several pairs at a time and always have some on hand when a cute baby needs some footwear.

FINISHED SIZE
Instructions are written for size Newborn-6 months. Changes for 6-12 months, 12-18 months, and 18-24 months are in parentheses.
Sole length: 2¾ (3¼, 3½, 4)" (7 [8.5, 9, 10] cm).

Shown in size 12-18 months.

YARN
Worsted weight (#4 Medium).

Shown here: Plymouth Yarn Encore Tweed (75% acrylic, 22% wool, 3% rayon; 200 yd [183 m]/3½ oz [100 g]): #0789 grey, 1 skein.

HOOK
Size G/6 (4 mm). *Adjust hook size if necessary to obtain correct gauge.*

NOTIONS
Stitch markers (m); yarn needle.

GAUGE
19 sts and 20 rows = 4" (10 cm) in sc, after blocking.

Sole (make 2)

Ch 8 (10, 12, 14).

Rnd 1: Sk first ch (counts as st), sl st in next 4 (5, 6, 7) ch, sc in next 3 (4, 5, 6) ch, 3 sc in slip knot and over top of tail at end of row, turn work 180 degrees to work in bottom ridge lp of ch, sc in next 3 (4, 5, 6) ch, sl st in next 4 (5, 6, 7) ch, sl st in beg ch to join in the rnd—18 (22, 26, 30) sts.

Rnd 2: Ch 1 (counts as st here and throughout), place marker (pm) to indicate beg of rnd, sc in previously unworked beg ch, 2 sc in next st, sc in next 6 (8, 10, 12) sts, 2 sc in each of next 3 sts, sc in next 6 (8, 10, 12) sts, 2 sc in next st, sl st in beg st to join—24 (28, 32, 36) sts.

Rnd 3: Ch 1, sc in next st, 2 sc in each of the next 2 sts, sc in next 4 (6, 8, 10) sts, hdc in next 2 sts, 2 hdc in each of the next 2 sts, sc in next 2 sts, 2 hdc in each of the next 2 sts, hdc in next 2 sts, sc in next 4 (6, 8, 10) sts, 2 sc in each of the next 2 sts, sl st in beg st to join—32 (36, 40, 44) sts.

Rnd 4: Ch 1, sc in next st, 2 sc in each of next 3 sts, sc in next 8 (10, 12, 14) sts, 2 sc in each of next 3 sts, sc in next 2 sts, 2 sc in each of next 3 sts, sc in next 8 (10, 12, 14) sts, 2 sc in each of next 3 sts, sl st in beg st to join—44 (48, 52, 56) sts. Fasten off.

Toe (make 2)

Ch 2.

Row 1: 4 sc in 2nd ch from hook, turn—4 sts.

Row 2: Ch 1 (does not count as st here and throughout), 2 sc in each st across, turn—8 sts.

Row 3: Ch 1, *sc in next sc, 2 sc in next sc, rep from * to end of row, turn—12 sc.

Row 4: Ch 1, *sc in next 2 sc, 2 sc in next sc, rep from * to end of row, turn—16 sc.

Row 5: Ch 1, *sc in next 3 sc, 2 sc in next sc, rep from * to end of row, turn—20 sc.

SIZES 0–6 (6–12) MONTHS ONLY

Row 6: Ch 1, *sc in next 4 sc, 2 sc in next sc, rep from * to end of row, ch 3 (4), turn—24 sc, 3 (4) ch.

Row 7: Sk first ch, sc in next 2 (3) ch and in each st across, ch 3 (4), turn—26 (27) sc, 3 (4) ch.

Row 8: Sk first ch, sc in next 2 (3) ch and in each st across—28 (30) sc. Fasten off.

SIZES 12–18 (18–24) MONTHS ONLY

Row 6: Ch 1, *sc in next 4 sc, 2 sc in next sc, rep from * to end of row, turn—24 sc.

SIZE 12–18 MONTHS ONLY

Row 7: Ch 1, *sc in next 5 sc, 2 sc in next sc, rep from * to end of row, ch 3, turn—28 sc, 3 ch.

Row 8: Sk first ch, sc in next 2 ch and in each st across, ch 3, turn—30 sc, 3 ch.

Row 9: Sk first ch, sc in next 2 ch and in each st across—32 sc. Fasten off.

SIZE 18–24 MONTHS ONLY

Row 7: Ch 1, *sc in next 5 sc, 2 sc in next sc, rep from * to end of row, turn—28 sc.

Row 8: Ch 1, *sc in next 6 sc, 2 sc in next sc, rep from * to end of row, ch 3, turn—32 sc, 3 ch.

Row 9: Sk first ch, sc in next 2 ch and in each st across, ch 3, turn—34 sc, 3 ch.

Row 10: Sk first ch, sc in next 2 ch and in each st across—36 sc. Fasten off.

Heel (make 2)

Make an adjustable ring (see Glossary).

Rnd 1: 14 sc in ring, sl st in beg st to join in the rnd, place marker to indicate beg of rnd, pull tail to close ring.

Rnd 2: Ch 1 (does not count as st here and throughout), *2 sc in next 5 sts, 2 dc in next 2 sts, rep from * to end of rnd, sl st in beg st to join—28 sts.

SIZES 0–6 (6–12) MONTHS ONLY

Fasten off.

SIZES 12–18 (18–24) MONTHS ONLY

Rnd 3: Ch 1, *[sc in next sc, 2 sc in next sc] 5 times, [dc in next dc, 2 dc in next dc] 2 times, rep from * to end of rnd, sl st in beg st to join—42 sts. Fasten off.

Finishing

With wrong sides facing, line up center of toe section to center front of sole. Pin edges tog using stitch markers or pins, and seam around edges with mattress st (see Glossary). Next, fold circular heel in half to obtain center edge. Line up center edge of heel with center back of sole. Pin edges of heel to wrong side of sole, with sides overlapping to the inside of the toe piece, and seam around edges. Seam side overlap securely, being careful not to let sts show through to RS. Fasten off. Weave in ends.

beg	begin; begins; beginning
bet	between
blo	back loop only
CC	contrasting color
ch(s)	chain(s)
cm	centimeter(s)
cont	continue(s); continuing
dc	double crochet
dec	decrease(s); decreasing; decreased
dtr	double treble crochet
est	established
flo	front loop only
fnd	foundation
foll	follows; following
g	gram(s)
hdc	half double crochet
inc	increase(s); increasing; increased
lp(s)	loop(s)
MC	main color
m	marker; meter(s)
mm	millimeter(s)
patt(s)	pattern(s)
pm	place marker
rem	remain(s); remaining
rep	repeat; repeating
rnd(s)	round(s)
RS	right side
sc	single crochet
sk	skip
sl	slip
sl st	slip(ped) stitch
sp(s)	space(s)
st(s)	stitch(es)
tog	together
tr	treble crochet
WS	wrong side
yd	yard(s)
yo	yarn over

* repeat starting point

() alternative measurements and/or instructions; work instructions within parentheses in place directed

[] work bracketed instructions a specified number of times

Glossary

MAKING AN ADJUSTABLE RING

Make a large loop with the yarn (figure 1). Holding the loop with your fingers, insert hook in loop and pull working yarn through loop (figure 2). Yarn over hook, pull through loop on hook. Continue to work indicated number of stitches in loop (figure 3; shown in single crochet). Pull on yarn tail to close loop (figure 4).

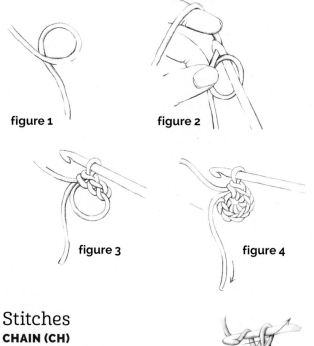

figure 1   figure 2

figure 3   figure 4

Stitches

CHAIN (CH)

Make a slipknot and place it on crochet hook. *Yarn over hook and draw through loop on hook. Repeat from * for the desired number of stitches.

HALF DOUBLE CROCHET (HDC)

*Yarn over, insert hook in stitch, yarn over and pull up loop (3 loops on hook), yarn over (figure 1) and draw through all loops on hook (figure 2); repeat from *.

figure 1   figure 2

DOUBLE CROCHET (DC)

*Yarn over hook, insert hook in a stitch, yarn over hook and draw up a loop **(figure 1)**—3 loops on hook, yarn over hook and draw it through 2 loops **(figure 2)**, yarn over hook and draw it through remaining 2 loops on hook **(figure 3)**. Repeat from *.

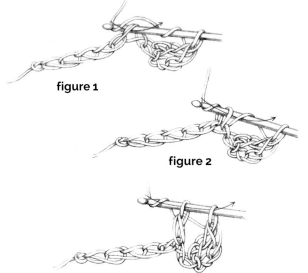

figure 1

figure 2

figure 3

TREBLE CROCHET (TR)

*Wrap yarn around hook twice, insert hook in next indicated stitch, yarn over hook and draw up a loop (4 loops on hook; **figure 1**), yarn over hook and draw it through 2 loops **(figure 2)**, yarn over hook and draw it through next 2 loops, yarn over hook and draw it through the remaining 2 loops on hook **(figure 3)**. Repeat from *.

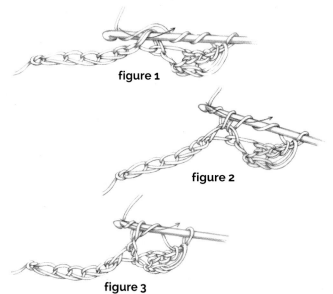

figure 1

figure 2

figure 3

REVERSE SINGLE CROCHET (REV SC)

Working from left to right, insert crochet hook in an edge stitch and pull up loop, yarn over and draw this loop through the first one to join, *insert hook in next stitch to right **(figure 1)**, pull up a loop, yarn over **(figure 2)**, and draw through both loops on hook **(figure 3)**; repeat from *.

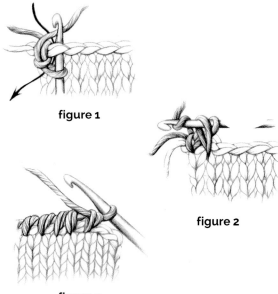

figure 1

figure 2

figure 3

FRONT POST DOUBLE CROCHET (FPDC)

Yarn over hook, insert hook from front to back to front around post of stitch indicated, yarn over hook and pull up a loop (3 loops on hook), [yarn over hook and draw through 2 loops on hook] twice—1 FPdc made.

FRONT POST TREBLE CROCHET (FPTR)

Yarn over hook twice, insert hook from front to back to front around post of stitch indicated, yarn over hook and pull up loop, [yarn over hook, draw through 2 loops on hook] 3 times—1 FPtr made.

Decreases

SINGLE CROCHET TWO TOGETHER (SC2TOG)

Insert hook in stitch, yarn over, and pull up a loop (2 loops on hook, **figure 1**). Insert hook in next stitch, yarn over, and up a loop (3 loops on hook). Yarn over hook and draw through all 3 loops on hook (**figure 2**)—1 stitch decreased (**figure 3**).

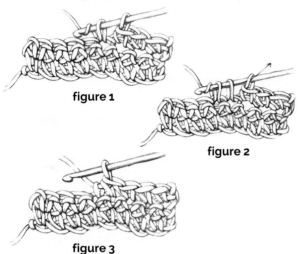

SINGLE CROCHET THREE TOGETHER (SC3TOG)

[Insert hook in next stitch, yarn over, pull loop through stitch] 3 times (4 loops on hook). Yarn over and draw yarn through all 4 loops on hook. Completed sc3tog—2 stitches decreased.

HALF DOUBLE CROCHET TWO TOGETHER (HDC2TOG)

[Yarn over hook, insert hook in next stitch, yarn over hook and pull up loop (**figure 1**)] twice, yarn over hook and draw through all loops on hook (**figure 2**)—1 stitch decreased (**figure 3**).

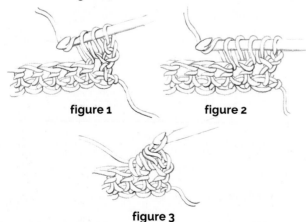

DOUBLE CROCHET TWO TOGETHER (DC2TOG)

[Yarn over, insert hook in next stitch, yarn over and pull up loop (**figure 1**), yarn over, draw through 2 loops] 2 times (**figure 2**), yarn over, draw through all loops on hook (**figure 3**)—1 stitch decreased (**figure 4**).

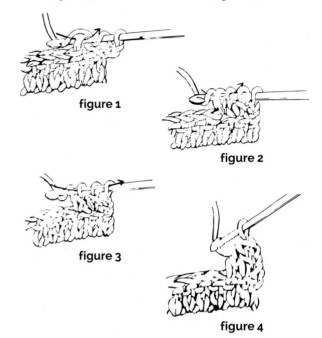

DOUBLE CROCHET THREE TOGETHER (DC3TOG)

[Yarn over, insert hook in next stitch, yarn over and pull up loop, yarn over, draw through 2 loops] 3 times (4 loops on hook), yarn over, draw through all loops on hook—2 stitches decreased.

Seaming and Joining

BACKSTITCH

Working from right to left, bring the needle up at **1** and insert behind the starting point at **2**. Bring the needle up at **3** (**figure 1**). Repeat by inserting at **1** and bringing the needle up at a point that is a stitch length beyond **3** (**figure 2**).

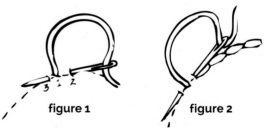

MATTRESS STITCH

Hold both pieces to be joined with the right sides facing and edges parallel to each other. Use threaded yarn needle to *insert the needle vertically under and out a stitch (or post) on the first piece and then under and out of the corresponding stitch (or post) of the second piece. Repeat from * to end of seam.

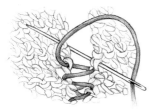

figure 1

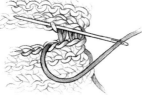

figure 2

WHIPSTITCH

With right sides (RS) of work facing and working through edge stitches, bring threaded needle out from back to front, along edge of piece.

Embroidery

FRENCH KNOT

Bring needle out of background from back to front, wrap yarn around needle 1 to 3 times and use thumb to hold in place while pulling needle through wraps into background a short distance from where it came out.

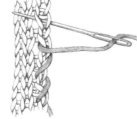

RUNNING STITCH

Working small straight stitches, pass the threaded needle over one crocheted stitch and under the next to form a dashed line. The stitches can be worked in equal or varying lengths, horizontally, vertically, or diagonally.

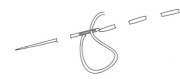

SATIN STITCH

Work closely spaced straight stitches, in graduated lengths as desired, and entering and exiting in the center of or at the side of the crocheted stitches.

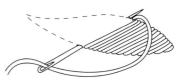

SLIP-STITCH (CROCHET CHAIN) EMBROIDERY

Holding yarn under background, insert hook through center of background, pull up loop, *insert hook into background a short distance away, pull 2nd loop up through the first loop on hook; repeat from *.

Pom-Poms

Cut two circles of cardboard, each ½" (1.3 cm) larger than desired finished pom-pom width. Cut a small circle out of the center and a small edge out of the side of each circle **(figure 1)**. Tie a strand of yarn between the circles, hold circles together and wrap with yarn—the more wraps, the thicker the pom-pom. Knot the tie strand tightly and cut between the circles **(figure 2)**. Place pom-pom between two smaller cardboard circles held together with a needle, and trim the edges **(figure 3)**.

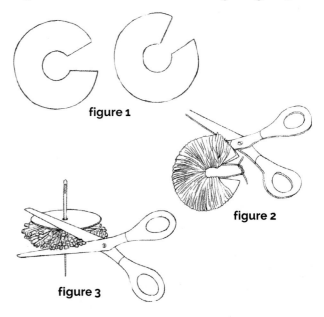

figure 1

figure 2

figure 3

Sources for Yarns

BERROCO
1 Tupperware Drive, Suite 4
North Smithfield, RI 02896
(401) 769-1212
berroco.com

BLUE SKY ALPACAS/
SPUD & CHLOË
PO Box 88
Cedar, MN 55011
(888) 460-8862
blueskyalpacas.com

BROWN SHEEP
100662 County Road 16
Mitchell, NE 69357
(800) 826-9136
brownsheep.com

CASCADE YARNS
cascadeyarns.com

CLASSIC ELITE YARNS
16 Esquire Road, Unit 2
North Billerica, MA 01862
(800) 343-0308
classiceliteyarns.com

HAZEL KNITS
hazelknits.com

LION BRAND YARNS
135 Kero Road
Carlstadt, NJ 07072
(800) 258-YARN
lionbrand.com

MADELINETOSH
7515 Benbrook Parkway
Benbrook, TX 76126
(817) 249-3066
madelinetosh.com

MALABRIGO YARN
(786) 866-6187
malabrigoyarn.com

MANOS DEL URUGUAY/
FAIRMOUNT FIBERS, LTD.
PO Box 2082
Philadelphia, PA 19103
(888) 566-9970
fairmountfibers.com

NEIGHBORHOOD
FIBER CO.
neighborhoodfiberco.com

O-WOOL
o-wool.com

PATONS/SPINRITE, LLC
320 Livingstone Avenue South, Box 40
Listowel, ON
Canada N4W 3H3
(888) 368-8401
yarnspirations.com/patons

PLYMOUTH YARN
COMPANY
500 Lafayette Street
Bristol, PA 19007
(215) 788-0459
plymouthyarn.com

ROWAN
+44 (0)1484 681881
knitrowan.com
USA: Westminster Fibers
165 Ledge St.
Nashua, NH 03060
(800) 445-9276
westminsterfibers.com

SCHUMTZERELLA YARNS
schmutzerellayarns.com

Acknowledgments

As always, a huge thank-you is due to all of the designers and yarn suppliers. I could not execute my vision without your beautiful creations. Thank you to Michelle Bredeson, Kerry Bogert, Jeannie Chin, and the entire team at Interweave. Your skills, advice, and encouragement are invaluable to the process. And finally, thank you to my family and friends. Your endurance when it comes to listening to rants about yarn and editing is admirable. Jesse, Nancy, Kassie, I love you all.

About the Designers

SHARON ZIENTARA

Author Sharon Zientara is a freelance crochet designer who has created designs for *Interweave Crochet* and *Interweave Crochet Accessories.* She is the former assistant editor at *Interweave Crochet* and former manager of Skacel's Makers' Mercantile in Seattle, Washington, and was a visual merchandiser for several large retailers. She is the author of *It Girl Crochet* and *3 Skeins or Less: Quick Crocheted Accessories.*

A LA SASCHA

A la Sascha is Sascha Blase, a Dutch crochet and knitting pattern designer with a wide range of different patterns, from amigurumi to accessories and clothing. Find more on alasascha.com.

BRENDA K. B. ANDERSON

Brenda K. B. Anderson is the author of *Beastly Crochet* and *Crochet Ever After.* Her designs have been published in numerous magazines including *Interweave Crochet* and *Crochet Today.* She has contributed to several books including *It Girl Crochet* and *Crochet at Home* (both from Interweave). Whimsical accessories, amigurumi, and other small projects are her absolute favorite things to design. She can be found on Ravelry as yarnville.

JANET BRANI

Janet Brani teaches and creates from her home studio in Marietta, Georgia. She enjoys the speed and freedom of crochet, and she designs with an eye toward simple construction and wearable fabric. In the social media arena, you will find her as OneLoopShy Designs.

ROBYN CHACHULA

Robyn Chachula is the author of *Blueprint Crochet Sweaters, Unexpected Afghans,* and *Crochet Stitches Visual Encyclopedia.* Her work has been featured in *Interweave Crochet, Crochet!, Love of Crochet, Vogue Crochet,* and more. She is one of the crochet experts on the PBS show *Knit and Crochet Now!* All of her crochet inspiration comes from her little ones at home in Pittsburgh, Pennsylvania. Stop by crochetbyfaye.com to see what she has cooked up recently.

TERRI L. KELLER

Terri Keller has been enjoying her crochet addiction for over thirty-five years now! Nothing brings her more pleasure than to design a pattern, dig through her yarn stash, and crochet up projects for her many grandbabies.

KATHY MERRICK

Kathy Merrick designs crochet and knitting patterns from her home on the Hudson River in Woodstock, New York. She's been designing for a number of years and still finds it riveting every day. Her work as appeared in *Interweave Crochet, Vogue Knitting, Vogue Knitting Crochet,* and other books and magazines.

CRISTINA MERSHON

Cristina Mershon is a graphic designer by day and crocheter by night. She was born in Spain, in the small region of Galicia, where handcrafting has been a tradition for centuries. She loves creating classic crochet pieces with a modern twist, simple and flattering shapes, and elaborate edgings.

KATYA NOVIKOVA

Katya Novikova lives in Moscow with her daughter, Maria. She started to crochet for her daughter when she was about six months old and very soon after, crocheting became her passion.

ANASTASIA POPOVA

Anastasia Popova's crochet career began when she designed and produced a line of kids' clothes and accessories for local boutiques. She enjoys sharing her crochet passion with others and teaches crochet classes in central New Jersey and eastern Pennsylvania. See her schedule of classes and catch up with her at anastasiapopova.com.

LISA VAN KLAVEREN

Lisa van Klaveren learned to crochet when she was three and grew up playing with her crochet hooks and teaching herself to read patterns. In her twenties, she designed and published a few baby blanket and afghan patterns. After becoming a stay-at-home mom in 2008, she began to design full-time and self-publish her designs on Etsy: hollanddesigns.etsy.com. The shop was named after her eldest daughter, Holland (her husband is half-Dutch). She lives in New Zealand with her three daughters and recently began her own quarterly crochet e-magazine, hollanddesignscrochet.com. She photographs her own designs, and her little girls are her inspiration and models.

Index

abbreviations 120

adjustable ring 120

backstitch 122

chain stitch (ch) 120

double crochet (dc) 121
double crochet three together (dc3tog) 122
double crochet two together (dc2tog) 122

embroidery stitches 123

French knot 123
front post double crochet (FPdc) 121
front post treble crochet (FPtr) 121

half double crochet (hdc) 120
half double crochet two together (hdc2tog) 122

joins 122–123

mattress stitch 123

pom-pom 123

reverse single crochet (rev sc) 121
running stitch 123

satin stitch 123
seams 122–123
single crochet three together (sc3tog) 122
single crochet two together (sc2tog) 122
slip-stitch (crochet chain) 123

treble crochet (tr) 121

whipstitch 123

Editor
MICHELLE BREDESON

Acquiring Editor
KERRY BOGERT

Technical Editor
JEANNIE CHIN

Art Direction and Design
CHARLENE TIEDEMANN

Photographer
JOE HANCOCK

Stylist
TINA GILL

Assistant Stylist & Baby Wrangler
JEFF ERWINE

Production Coordinator
BRYAN DAVIDSON

METRIC CONVERSION CHART

TO CONVERT:	TO:	MULTIPLY BY:
Inches	Centimeters	2.54
Centimeters	Inches	0.4
Feet	Centimeters	30.5
Centimeters	Feet	0.03
Yards	Meters	0.9
Meters	Yards	1.1

a content + ecommerce company

www.fwcommunity.com

20 19 18 17 16   5 4 3 2 1

Distributed in Canada by Fraser Direct
100 Armstrong Avenue
Georgetown, ON, Canada L7G 5S4
Tel: (905) 877-4411

Distributed in the U.K. and Europe by F&W MEDIA INTERNATIONAL
Brunel House, Newton Abbot, Devon, TQ12 4PU, England
Tel: (+44) 1626 323200, Fax: (+44) 1626 323319
E-mail: enquiries@fwmedia.com

Distributed in Australia by Capricorn Link
P.O. Box 704, S. Windsor NSW, 2756 Australia
Tel: (02) 4560 1600, Fax: (02) 4577 5288
E-mail: books@capricornlink.com.au

SRN: 16CRO3
ISBN-13: 978-1-63250-217-9

We make every effort to ensure the accuracy of our instructions, but mistakes occasionally occur. Errata can be found at **crochetme.com/errata.**

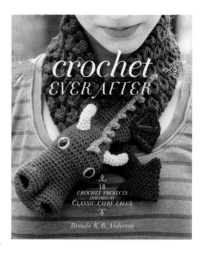